Praise for Ask Witho

MW00577478

"Ask Without Fear for Ch
musician, entrepreneur a.
for money and when I eventually do so, I'm convinced I do it all wrong.
I don't want to extend my own kingdom, I want to extend God's kingdom. The truth is that I often need resources to do so but have no idea
at all how to manage the process of asking people to partner with me
financially. I'm very thankful for the hard work and passionate dedica-
tion Marc has given to giving me the heart and mind help that I need
in this crucial area."

Paul Colman singer/songwriter/producer/communicator

"Ask Without Fear for Christian Ministry *is a fun and practical guide
that helps ministries get excited about inviting people to fund Kingdom
work. Marc reminds us that what we do as fundraisers isn't for short
term gain; our work aims towards eternal impact.* Ask Without Fear
for Christian Ministry, *isn't just about applicable concepts, it's a reminder that we should be passionate about what we do because it's a
calling that God's drawn us to.*"

Cyndi Whitecotton
Behavior Researcher, K-LOVE & Air1

"*Christian ministries often rely on 'bake sale' fundraising and are reluctant to engage in major gift solicitation because it's perceived as too unseemly or too difficult. Marc Pitman breaks down that resistance. For
those who find soliciting major gifts to be difficult, he provides meaningful, relevant, and practical guidance to assist fundraising staff and
volunteers in making that all-important ask. For those ministries that
find major gift fundraising to be unseemly, Marc demonstrates that asking for the support of others is not just how we fund our mission; it is an
inextricable part of our mission, woven throughout Scripture.*"

Dan McCormack
President, Hospital Sisters of St. Francis Foundation

"In a conversation with my pastor, he asked, 'What do I need to know to be confident, to make the ask, to do my best?' The points in this question are exactly the ones that Marc A. Pitman addresses in Ask Without Fear for Christian Ministry. *We first need [to] understand that the ask is not about the asker but about the mission, that the asker is an emissary of God's kingdom seeking further impact as opportunities arise, that opening up these opportunities to prospective donors will help them meet their personal aspirations and goals to invest their money wisely. Marc is a master at using his email blasts, blogging and speaking engagements to garner the needs and interests of thousands of fundraisers and donors across North America. From this interaction he has distilled the seminal points that are the focus of this book. Pick it up and learn a lot. REAL-ly!"*

D.C. Dreger, ACFRE
DC Dreger Associates

Praise for *Ask Without Fear for Librarians*

"Ask Without Fear for Librarians is an excellent confidence builder. I'm eager to see libraries around the country put its strategy into practice."

Sonja Plummer Morgan
Immediate Past President, Association for Rural & Small Libraries

"Ask Without Fear for Librarians is very practical. With all of the financial pressure on libraries, municipal funding cutbacks and small, aging 'Friends' groups, libraries need to learn how to be effective at fundraising. Reading this inspired me to make three calls yesterday and today, using your advice, and the results were great!"

James Wilkins
Director of Development, Auburn Public Library

"Using Marc's framework, we were able to exceed our fundraising goal in the worst recession since the Great Depression."

Sarah Sugden
Library Director, Waterville Public Library

Praise for *Ask Without Fear!*®

"GREAT training tool for helping those who are afraid to ask. Works like a charm … I was training a group of individuals at a parish site and used Ask Without Fear! We did some role-playing and during that, a couple volunteered to play the role of donor. When the exercise was over—they made a real pledge of $30,000. Thank you for sharing and God Bless You."

Theresa Montminy, Director
Office of Mission Advancement
Roman Catholic Diocese of San Bernardino

"Get REAL will take on new meaning for board and staff members who read this book. Readable, on point, filled with memorable stories and well-tested practices, this little book is a great addition to the field of pragmatic advice to those looking for more successful engagement in fundraising."

Kay Sprinkel Grace,
Principal, Transforming Philanthropy and
author, *Beyond Fundraising*

"I enjoyed Ask Without Fear! Marc has taken a subject that has been written about often and given it a new twist. Clearly, his effort is a work of passion and love. My hat is off to him."

Jerry Linzy
Senior Managing Partner, Panas, Linzy & Associates

"This short, practical book gives you a series of step-by-step methods to raise more money, faster and easier than you ever thought possible."

Brian Tracy
Author, *The Psychology Of Selling*

Other books by Marc A. Pitman

Ask Without Fear!®

Ask Without Fear for Librarians

The Ask Without Fear! DVD set

The Ask Without Fear! DVD Board Retreat-in-a-box set

Creating Donor Evangelists: Moving Donors from Mere Check Writers to Raving Fans

Fundraising Kick: A year of ask kicking ideas

Google+ for Nonprofits

The $100,000 Guide to E-mail Solicitation

The MagnetGoals Goal Setting Workbook

Nonprofit Social Media: A beginner's guide

Who's Telling Your Story?

Ask Without Fear
for Christian Ministry

Ask Without Fear
for Christian Ministry

Helping You Connect Donors with Causes
That Have Eternal Impact

Marc A. Pitman

Ask Without Fear for Christian Ministry
Published by Standish & Wade Publishing

© 2017 by The Concord Leadership Group, LLC

Cover Design by Joshua Fisher
joshuafish@gmail.com
Interior Design by Redbrush.com

ISBN-13: 978-1-938079-08-5 (print)
ISBN-13: 978-1-938079-09-2 (ebook)

For more information, or to purchase in bulk for your team, contact:
The Concord Leadership Group LLC
2435 East North Street
Suite 1108-171
Greenville, SC 29615
www.FundraisingCoach.com

To my wife, Emily, who—besides Jesus—is the best thing that's ever happened to this disciple!

Ask Without Fear for Christian Ministry

Foreword

Fear is a curious emotion. It's frequently surrounded by a lot of apparent contradictions.

Scripture tells us that we are to fear no one but God. However, when humans in the Bible encounter God or one of his messengers, that command seems almost superfluous. Time after time, the first words spoken by the divine being are, "Fear not." I assume this is because the human response is basically terror. Other times the overwhelming fear shows up as a deep sense of unworthiness in the presence of the Holy (Isaiah 6:5; Luke 5:8).

David is probably the biblical author who talks the most about fear. His psalms are filled with raw emotion describing his own struggles with fear juxtaposed with his confidence in God's protection and deliverance. In the New Testament, Jesus himself can be heard telling people, "Do not fear, only believe."

As Christ-followers we love to turn to these scriptural promises in times of fear. We quote them, memorize them, and put them on plaques or Post-it notes to remind us of God's protection. Acting on these promises has even moved Christians to do amazing things for the Kingdom in the face of great danger.

Yet somehow, when it comes to talking about money, the promises seem to lose their power.

Over my years of coaching ministry workers in fundraising, I've seen gifted, articulate leaders preach the gospel and boldly ask people to give their whole lives to following Jesus. But when faced with asking a friend to give to the work of God's Kingdom, those same leaders will stammer, apologize, and look at the ground. I've watched missionaries, who were confident in their call and willing to give up comfort and convenience to serve God, generate unending reasons why they couldn't pick up the phone to call a donor prospect.

Often the fear is rooted in shame or guilt. Other times it is tied to a fear of risking a relationship. And lots of times it comes out of our personal insecurity. The result, however, is always the same—ministry suffers because of a lack of resources.

Marc is passionate about helping us reframe those feelings to move beyond our fears. Through good preparation, a confident invitation, and joyful partnership, he shows us how to apply what we believe about God to our fundraising. And the result is that we truly can learn to "fear not"—even as we ask!

Donna Wilson
National Director of Ministry Partnership Development
InterVarsity Christian Fellowship/USA

Acknowledgments

The ongoing success of *Ask Without Fear!* has been truly heart-warming. It's amazing to see people realize that they can indeed ask for money. The book has inspired thousands of people to do exponentially more good in the world.

I truly wouldn't have written the first *Ask Without Fear!* without my faith in God. As a teenager, I started consciously following Jesus and have been fervent ever since. Figuring out how to faithfully fundraise was at the root of my development career. My first two jobs were at a Christian college and a Christian boarding/day school. When YouVersion came out, now called "The Bible App," its creators even asked me to put my "Fundraising in the Bible" devotional as one of their first 100 reading plans.

The Ask Without Fear!® System has been taught from lay leaders in groups like CLIMB (Christian Leaders in Maine Business) to more than 100 missionary fundraising coaches at the "Funding Your Ministry Symposium" on the Navigators' campus, and groups like the National Catholic Development Conference and the Diocese of Orange County. Individual church planters have hired me to help them, as have large ministries with over $100 million in revenue. Time and again, they are surprised by the joy I feel in our ministry of fundraising. And they start catching a bit of that joy too.

I'm thankful for the people that have encouraged me in this over the years. Bob Grinnell gave me principles that provided a solid foundation in raising money for the Kingdom. He also encouraged me over the years as I built upon those fundamental ideas. And leaders like Kathy Sides, Sr. Georgette Lehmuth, and Whitney Kuniholm have guided and challenged me through their example and their writings. I hesitate to list more because there have been so many, both Jesus-followers and not, who've been used by God to shape my path. But one more group deserves thanks: the congregation that for four years was

The Vineyard Church of Waterville. I loved planting and pastoring the church with you. I can't wait until eternity to see the fruit of all that God did amongst us.

I'm particularly grateful to Nancy Swanson, Jon Swanson, Hope Swanson, and Kim Moody Calderon for proofreading versions of this book. Their corrections and comments make this much stronger.

Of course, my wife, Emily, continues to deserve special mention. She inspires me, challenges me, and continues to endure me. And, after 21 years of marriage, she continues to be my best friend.

My kids deserve special thanks too. They have been very supportive of my writing and speaking. Thanks, guys! I'm proud to be your dad.

A note on the gender use of pronouns. I strive to be gender inclusive in life. Unfortunately, early readers of this work told me that my attempt to be gender inclusive in this writing made it very difficult to read. To fix that, I have chosen to use feminine pronouns in one chapter, then masculine in the next. I hope that shows both inclusiveness with an ease of reading.

As always, this work has had the input of many, but any errors in it are solely mine. In fact, since I know so many readers like to find errors, I may have put a few in there just for you!

Here's to making your sure your ministry gets fully funded!

Marc A. Pitman
Easter 2016

"Most of the people are very wonderful indeed, they almost always wish to do the right thing, and their ultimate performance, when boldly challenged and confidently led, is usually far better than we have any right to expect. Study them and treat them well, for you need them more than money."

Harold J. Seymour

Introduction
Can you be a Christian and ask for money?

At the start of my teenage years, my parents recommitted their lives to Jesus. A few years later, my sister and I also committed our lives to Him. (My parents will tell you we did it when they did; my sister and I will tell you it didn't "take" until later!) My parents made sure our family was immersed in Bible study and learning about our faith. They supported us in taking risks and growing in leadership, both in ministries and in secular areas like the boarding school we both attended.

But some things are more successfully "caught" than "taught." Both of my parents were generous and giving—my dad in particular. He didn't talk much about giving; he has always modeled it with his life. During one of the few times I remember him actually talking about giving, he gave a challenge to the congregation that allowed us a glimpse into his faith life. He suggested to us that tithing involved 10% of our *resources*, not just our money. "What if you took that seriously and went beyond tithing just your money? Tithing time would be about 2½ hours every day! Imagine what we could accomplish for God!"

I didn't realize how hardwired tithing and generosity was until my newly married wife and I sat down with my dad's business partner. He was helping us sort out the mess I had made of our finances.

At that point, I was giving 14% or so but going into debt in other areas. He pointed at the 14% and said, "Charity is nice, but yours needs to go down until you can afford to be that generous. Now, I know your dad so I know you won't go below 10%. I'd normally tell others to give much less, but I know that would be lost on you."

For me, tithing was definitely non-negotiable.

Right after getting married, I went to work as an admissions counselor at Gordon College, a Christian liberal arts college on the North Shore of Boston. I had recently graduated from Gordon, having created an honors program to prepare me to be a cross-cultural church planter. I loved the college; so recruiting was easy.

As an admissions counselor, I helped teenagers explore their talents, abilities, passions, and interests and helped them decide if Gordon was a good fit for God's call on their life. It was disappointing when those wonderful conversations ended after the student made their college decision.

After a couple of years at Gordon, I moved into donor development, and I've never looked back. In fundraising, I found I got to have the same conversations about passions and values, but the conversations didn't need to end after a few months. I was able to have them over years.

These conversations were definitely ministry. I've found that fundraising has opened doors to communities and community leaders that would not have opened if I were seen as a "minister." As I've spoken to audiences of nonprofits around the world, I've found there are lots of Jesus followers in fundraising work. It makes sense—Christians "get" the need to be generous!

Since I wrote *Ask Without Fear!*, I have been in many conversations with pastors, missionaries, and other Jesus followers needing help with fundraising. I've spoken in churches and to conferences of fundraising coaches, served on boards of different ministries, and worked with congregations on stewardship campaigns. In the early 2000's, I got to teach on stewardship, money, and giving as a pastor of a Vineyard church plant in rural Maine. I've studied fundraising stories in the Bible and was honored to have my work included as one of the first 100 reading plans on the YouVersion Bible app.

I truly believe Jesus is the hope of the world. And I believe that fundraising allows us to minister this hope to people in powerful ways.

I think it's so exciting when God calls us to invite people to fund the advancement of His Kingdom!

I have discovered not everyone shares my enthusiasm. Even people involved in ministry dread fundraising and never learn to do it well.

I am writing this simple guide to help you fund your ministry. I want to help you get over your fear of asking and see it as the amazing privilege it is. This book is for "normal" people trying to raise money for the Kingdom.

I know this system works. I have seen success in the lives of pastors, church planters, missionaries, and board members around the world.

Getting your ministry fully funded is not a spectator sport. Even George Mueller, famous for only asking God for money, *told people about God's provision.* These stories of provision let others know that his ministry was supported by donations! In his terrific book *Funding Your Ministry,* Scott Morton writes that George Mueller was incredibly money savvy. He was also quite deceitful before meeting God. So Mueller's way of experiencing God's provision (not manipulating people but relying on God) was not a formula for the church but an approach tailored to his own personal spiritual growth.

For many, the bad news is that fully funding your ministry requires *asking*. The Bible is full of fundraising stories. People like Moses, David, Hezekiah, Nehemiah, and Paul all asked for money to support ministry. People do not think of these saints as any less "godly" for asking. One of the great things about looking at fundraising in the Bible is that when people give, a worship session tends to break out. And on more than one occasion the people have to be told to stop giving! I haven't yet experienced that outpouring, but I keep hoping the next solicitation will result in such a revival!

Fortunately, asking for money is one of the most natural things to do. It is all about connecting your story to the donor's story.

1. You *identify* who is most likely to respond well to your mission. (Different people will respond to different aspects.)

2. You *listen* to their story.

3. You *show* them points of intersection with your mission.

4. You *ask* if they would consider investing in one of those points of intersection.

5. You *thank* them either way and repeat the process with the next person.

I like to call fundraising an "extreme sport"—all the adrenaline rush of bungee jumping but no risk of falling. There's nothing quite like the rush of helping people connect their finances with their passions. It's like putting a plug into a socket: electric! It is even more thrilling when you know that wherever the donors may be on their spiritual journeys, they are investing for eternal impact!

That is why I wrote this book. I want to help you recapture the excitement that brought you into ministry in the first place. This is for paid employees, people raising their own support, and volunteers who see a need that requires funding.

I will show you some of the secrets to successfully asking for money in a way that will put the "fun" back into fundraising. Instead of dreading fundraising and viewing it as a necessary evil, you will learn how to connect not only with potential donors' checkbooks but also with their lives. As you discover the passions and the stories at the core of your donors, you may be surprised at what you find. That discovery may be even greater than simply funding your ministry's latest and greatest project.

I'm a firm believer in keeping things simple — especially in fundraising. So I've distilled the process of successful fundraising to the acronym "R.E.A.L.":

- Research
- Engage
- Ask
- Love

If you have tried to follow a fundraising program before, you know it can make you feel like a human pretzel; you have to bend yourself in unnatural ways only getting twisted up in knots. I want to help you unwind and be yourself— the person God created you to be. You don't have to learn some sort of "schpeal." You don't have to manipulate people. Being yourself and linking your passion for ministry with something they value will be the most effective way to raise lots of money and community support.

In this book, you will laugh at some of the biggest mistakes made when fundraising. You will learn a simple way to make sure your materials connect with donors. You will be introduced to some assessments that will help you learn to communicate more effectively with donors and colleagues. I will also share with you my insights as we study some stories of fundraising in the Bible.

These tools will help your current donors and fans have concrete ways to attract new donors. All the stories here are real, but some details have been changed to protect the people involved.

The process of fundraising is exciting, especially when you are equipped to do it correctly. Not only can you be a Christian and ask for money, but you can also bring others further into the Kingdom in more ways than you thought possible. Fundraising really is ministry. So, let's start getting equipped!

Chapter 1
Research

"Suppose one of you wants to build a tower. Won't you first sit down and estimate the cost to see if you have enough money to complete it?"
                    - Jesus, Luke 14:28 (NIV)

"Fundraising is the gentle art of teaching the joy of giving."
                    - Hank Rosso

"Donors don't give to institutions. They invest in ideas and people in whom they believe."
                    - G.T. Smith

"Action precedes funding Planning precedes action."
                    - Unknown

"In good times and bad, we
know that people give because
you meet needs, not because
you have needs."
                                            - Kay Sprinkel Grace

"Research is the process of going
up alleys to see if they are blind."
                                            - Marston Bates

"If we knew what it was we were
doing, it would not be called
research, would it?"
                                            - Albert Einstein

Do you enjoy asking for money? I absolutely love it!

Being a fundraiser is like holding an electric cord and facing a wall of outlets. Some of the outlets are 3-pronged, some are 2-pronged, some are 2-pronged with a wide side, some are curved like those used for a washer/dryer, and some are shaped like a Christmas tree (like the ones in New Zealand). The cord represents the donor; the wall of outlets represents the various aspects of your ministry. Your job is to get to know the donor well enough to determine which outlet to plug her into. When you plug it in by asking for the gift, *bang!* The electricity starts to flow!

Most people don't get to do as soul-satisfying work as fundraisers do. Many people simply have a job to pay the bills. Your asking helps them realize that what they work 40, 60, or 80 hours a week doing can actually be used to invest in something they value. You're helping them redeem the rest of their week by adding value to what they spend most of their lives doing.

When you see a donor's eyes light up with the joy that giving gives her, you'll get hooked!

The first time I asked for money as a development officer was electrifying for me. My mentor had intended to take me on solicitations, but it wasn't happening. So, I researched my first solicitation and set up the appointment.

A parent of a student was involved in a fatal accident the previous year while on a business trip. So my strategy was to ask the surviving parent to request a six-figure gift from the company that had employed his wife. The purpose of the donation would be to help construct part of our newest building which would be named in memory of her. The project was an exciting match of the donor's family interests with the organization's strategic priorities.

I went to the person's house, had a wonderful time visiting, and steered the conversation toward "the ask." It felt pretty natural. He said he would think about it. I felt elated.

Not until I returned to my office did I realize I had asked him on the anniversary of his wife's accident. Can you imagine how awful I felt? I had done research, but I hadn't done *enough* research! Not surprisingly, we didn't get that gift. But fortunately, we didn't lose his relationship either. In fact, he seemed far less disturbed about the whole thing than I was. I think he was impressed by my thoughtful attempt to match his family's interests with a pre-determined need on campus.

Even with that embarrassing experience, I knew I was hooked. The fundraising bug had bitten me. Trying to match the donor's interests (the electric cord) and the organization's pre-established strategic priorities (the outlets) was wonderful! I knew I was possibly helping this donor make a meaningful connection to something that mattered to him.

However, after talking with colleagues and clients over the years, I realize that most people aren't as eager to ask for money as I am. My work with them leads me to believe that most of this is fear of the unknown. This is often expressed in terms of "What if ... " questions:

- What if I offend the prospect?
- What if I embarrass myself?
- What if they question my motives?
- What if they ask me a question I can't answer?

What if ... ? What if ... ? What if ... ? God has blessed you with a great imagination. But using the imagination this way (imagining bad possibilities) helps no one.

Most people aren't brought up asking for money other than from their parents, so they think they have to transform into somebody else when they do ask. Unfortunately, some of the most visible Christian fundraisers use distasteful and sometimes unethical methods (hyping people up or manipulating through guilt) when asking for money. Who wants to be like that?

The good news is you can be yourself and still be a successful fundraiser!

To help you learn how, I suggest you need to begin by getting "R.E.A.L."—*Research, Engage, Ask,* and *Love.* This simple four-step formula is designed to help you get as excited about asking for money as I am. In the rest of this chapter, we'll investigate the first step: *research.*

Research

Most people seem to be afraid of asking for money because they don't have a clue how the prospective donor will respond. Let me show you how research (doing your homework before you ask) helps conquer this fear.

Michael Wyland of a consulting firm in South Dakota told me about a nonprofit organization asking a multi-billion dollar company to become a corporate sponsor of a duck race. This company was a perfect prospect for the nonprofit. It made sense that they'd be willing to give. But the duck race coordinators only asked them for $250! The company did become a sponsor, but at a far lower level than they were capable of giving. The organizers had no idea what this corporation was worth! They hadn't done their homework. They could have asked for much more. Now it will be very hard to go to this company next year and ask for a gift of $25,000.

Everyone makes mistakes like this from time to time. It's inevitable no matter how well you know your stuff. This is especially true when fundraising for Christian causes. You want to make sure everyone feels welcome to participate, so you end up going in with no strategy and wondering why passing the hat didn't work. Many people have a really hard time asking for more than they feel they can personally give. Fortunately, doing some simple research will get you over that fear.

Research Your Goal First

I'm shocked at how many ministries don't have a good answer to the question, "*How much are you trying to raise?*".

One would naturally think "more is better." The more money you raise, the better you'll be able to serve your community. But you can't structure your fundraising that way. You must decide on a firm goal. If you don't have a dollar goal, one way to start is by writing out a "case statement." I like to think of a case statement as what you'd say if you were called in before a court of law to argue the veracity of your fundraising. Your "case" for why it is worth investing in your cause.

In this, you'll want to put your stats. Things like, but not limited to:

- What are you trying to do? Include both theological and practical, hands-on perspectives. Theological: "We're preaching the Gospel of Jesus." Practical: "We're making sure everyone has access to digital tools and social media."

- Any statistics: How many are being fed? How many wells are being drilled? How many people is your outreach impacting?

- How many people come through your doors?

- How many access you through your website?

- How many reference questions do you answer each year (or month)?

- What kind of programs does your ministry run?
- What service is being provided for your community?
  - Social connections for seniors might increase health outcomes and reduce medical bills.
  - Free counseling and space for drug addicts or alcoholic meetings might bring down the ultimate cost that would otherwise be passed on to your city or region.
  - Are you providing services to people outside of your ministry or church? What are you doing? (Some are chaplains for the fire department. Others run soup kitchens. Or medical clinics. Or car tune-up clinics. Or movie nights.)
- Why is now the time for this ministry?
- What demographic trends indicate this is a great cause to back?
- What makes you unique from the existing ministries?

Just start describing what you do and imagining what others would say you've done for them. Put all of this down on paper.

Be sure to add the stories of people who benefit from the work. Use stories to back up the statistics. To fundraise effectively, you must speak to both the head (stats) and the heart (emotions).

You should also get "social proof." Studies show that people are more likely to support a cause if they see proof that others like them support it. So in your case statement, get quotes from:

- Leaders in your community or cause area
- Board members
- People you've supported or ministered to

- Donors who've already contributed
- Outside groups that find your work and ministry invaluable in carrying out their mission

Pictures are a powerful way to give "social proof." So take pictures. I'd even recommend getting a simple video camera (like the one in your cell phone) and asking for 30-second comments. Ask the people who benefit from your work what they like most about your ministry. Be sure to tell them this will be used online and in print. If you need to, you can distribute permission slips for the use of the photos (especially for minors!) and collect and file the completed slips. People are often flattered to be asked. And these quick videos will lend themselves well to posting online or pulling still shots out for print publications.

As you're writing out your case statement, jot down how much it costs to do each aspect of your ministry. Finding those numbers should be easy. Look at your annual costs. Include what maintenance would cost if you fixed things when they broke instead of deferring it. Remember to include the costs of the people staffing the outreach. If you're raising your own salary, be sure to include the appropriate percentages for savings, retirement, college funds, etc.

That number may be too overwhelming for one fundraising campaign, but the research will be invaluable for your fundraising, marketing, community relations, town/city relations, and talks to churches and service groups.

Two last things to remember as you rework your case statement

(1) Keep it jargon-free

(2) Sell benefits, not features

Keep it jargon-free
Many people motivated to go into missions are so passionate that

they've spent a lot of time studying the theology of their approach. You might even have gone to school, earned advanced degrees, and become very literate in your field. But most of your donors haven't. Your goal in fundraising is to involve people whose lives *don't* revolve around your ministry. To do that, you need to translate jargon for them. How do you know if you're using jargon?

Read it out loud.
Seriously. Read the case out loud. Not skimming, murmuring reading. Print-it-out-and-read-it-as-though-you-were-speaking-to-someone reading. Have a pen or pencil handy to put a simple check next to areas you stumble over. Don't fix those areas right now; you'll come back and do that later. Just read it through and notice what might need explaining.

Get someone unfamiliar with your ministry or project to read it.
This is the best way to keep any of your communications jargon free. Many authors suggest writing at a sixth-grade level (something a 12-year-old would understand). Remember, you're not trying to win any literary awards with this case, and you're not trying to impress your high school English teacher. *You're trying to incite action.* To do that, you must be clear and direct. Having a person outside your immediate circle read it will help you immensely.

Share benefits, not features

Many training programs talk about the difference between features and benefits. Features are the steak and the pan; benefits are the sizzle and smell. Your strategy for ministry is a feature. The resulting changed lives are the benefits. Leading with your meeting times or the sources of your material can cause a potential donor to appropriately say, "So what." Those who are outside of your head have nothing to which they can compare that number. You need to translate it into terms they understand.

One of the biggest mistakes you can make is bragging about your nonprofit or ministry. You may do it with the best of intentions. If you're asking people to give you money, you feel the need to prove that your organization is a good investment. But talking all about you is about as interesting as going on a date with a person who only talks about herself. It is b-o-r-i-n-g.

It is more compelling to talk about transformed lives, protected land, or the unexpected impact the Kingdom is having in unlikely sectors of society. If you're pastoring a congregation, it is good to talk about the discipline of giving—not in a manipulative way, but as a mark of a follower of Jesus. I heard my pastor say something like this during a campaign:

> "We don't need your money. God is calling us to this vision, and it's up to Him to fund it. And God doesn't need your money. He owns 'the cattle on a thousand hills.' But God knows how closely your heart is tied to your wallet, so He expects His followers to be generous."

A great way to think about the features/benefits conversation was summed up by the phrase, "sell the sizzle, not the steak." Sales guru Zig Ziglar loved pointing out that millions of drills are sold each year. But no one wants a drill. They want a hole. The drill is the feature; the hole—the end result—is the benefit. What is the result that your project aims to make a reality? Talk about that!

Get to work making sure your case statement not only has all the facts but also helps people translate what those facts mean for the Kingdom and for their own journey.

Free Online Tools

Now that you have a specific number, it would be very tempting to divide that evenly. If you're trying to raise $100,000, it's very easy to fall into the "we-just-need-to-get-$100-from-1000-people" mindset. I've even heard some people look to Biblical stories for the numbers of supporters:

- 12 disciples or tribes of Israel
- 70 people Jesus sent out
- 120 people at Pentecost
- 300 people in Gideon's army
- 144,000 mentioned in Revelation

This makes sense mathematically and makes inspiring stories to tell, but *decades of fundraising research show that money doesn't come that way.* One of the great tools for you to use is a gift range calculator. There are a few on the web, one of them is at: www.GiftRangeCalculator.com.

For instance, to raise $100,000, most gift tables will say you'll need to have the first gift be 10%-25% of the goal, i.e. $10,000-$25,000. The next three should add up to another 25%, maybe one at $15,000 and a couple at $7,500. Personally, I prefer to be more conservative. I'd look for the first gift to be 25% to 50% of goal. (Google "gift range calculators" to find other calculators that use the less conservative, but equally reliable numbers.)

www.GiftRangeCalculator.com

Target Amount: 1000000   calculate

GIFT RANGE	# GIFTS REQ.	# PROSPECTS REQ.	SUBTOTAL	CUMULATIVE TOTAL	CUMULATIVE %
250000	1	5	250000	250000	25%
150000	1	5	150000	400000	40%
100000	2	10	200000	600000	60%
75000	2	10	150000	750000	75%
50000	3	15	150000	900000	90%
25000	4	20	100000	1000000	100%
20000	6	30	120000	1120000	112%
10000	8	40	80000	1200000	120%
5000	10	50	50000	1250000	125%
2500	12	60	30000	1280000	128%
Total:	49	245		1280000	

You'll notice the total adds up to over 100%. This is intentional.
(1) Costs of construction always tend to go up.
(2) Nonprofits often neglect to budget donor recognition in their plans.
Plaques and signs always add up to more than we expect.
(3) It's always better to raise more than you need.

An example of a $100,000 gift range chart from www.GiftRangeCalculator.com.

Take a look at the example chart. Can you see that you need four or five prospects with the ability to make that gift at each level? Using the example above, you'd need five prospects able to make the $25,000 gift and 15 to make the next three gifts.

Fundraising expert Jerry Linzy of Jerry Panas, Linzy & Partners told me, "Our experience demonstrates you need three or four probable donors to secure the gift. We also prefer the lead gift to be 15% to 20%, not 10%. We find today that the top 20 to 50 gifts need to represent half the goal."

This fact is worth the price of this book!

Now that you know how many names you need at each level, start filling them in. Who are five people or companies or foundations that might be able to make the first gift? Then list the next five for the next gift and continue down the chart.

If you want, you can make the gifts be boxes and form them into a gift pyramid. Not all the boxes need to be filled in by donors. Fundraising events, direct mail programs, or things like sales of Fair Trade goods can fill in some of them.

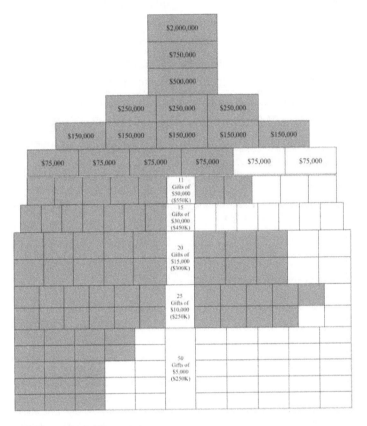

(Shaded areas reflect gifts/pledges received)
An example of a gift pyramid for a $7 million campaign.

Now that you have those names (those potential prospects), how do you find out if they are actual prospects capable of making that level of gift to your ministry?

One of the best tools for this kind of homework is probably one you're already using: *Google*. Type the name of the person you want to approach in the Google search box and see what comes up. It's pretty amazing how much public information is out there on people.

It may be helpful to put her name in quotes and spell out the state or country she lives in to narrow the search. You may include her name and "trustees" or "donors" to see if she's included on nonprofit boards or donor lists. Be sure to look at political giving, too. Jesus' disciples ranged from religious conservatives looking to overthrow the Roman occupation (Judas Iscariot) to collaborators with the Romans (Matthew). God also used pagan emperors like Cyrus and Artaxerxes to fund building projects. So be open to God supplying your needs from all corners.

What's really fun is pulling up information that is out of the ordinary. You may find a book review that a person made or a blog post she wrote. While those things shouldn't necessarily be mentioned during your visit, you will have a much clearer picture of the person when you meet with her.

Be careful not to rely on Google alone! A few years ago, if you typed in my name, half the sites that come up for "Marc Pitman" are for a guy who starred in horror movies with names like "Roadkill" and "Deadbeat at Dawn." It's a riot, but it's not me (I hope no one thinks it *is* me ...)! So, please be sure to take your Google findings with a grain of salt.

For a treasure trove of similar online research tools, check out the University of Vermont's Research Tools Page http://www.uvm.edu/~prospect/index.html

With all the web-based tools, don't forget the good, old-fashioned donor files. If you have a history of philanthropy, it's helpful to look at those records on a somewhat regular basis. At some places I've worked, they had file cabinets stuffed with records going back to the 1930s! You will find some fascinating information about prospects in those notes!

Outsourcing Research

Another way to research is to send all your database information to a vendor that specializes in prospect research and modeling. Groups like DonorTrends, DonorSearch, WealthEngine, iWave and Blackbaud's Target Analytics do this all the time. They have access to large amounts of public information, and they have formulas for knowing how to quantify that information. This analysis can be incredibly valuable to you, even on a project as simple as a mailing. By using this type of service, I cut my annual fund mailings from an entire database of 14,000 records to just mailing the 4,000 most likely to make a gift. I raised just as much money but saved a bundle in production and postage!

Peer Reviews & The CPI Index

One of the most effective and least expensive ways of researching prospective donors is *asking other people*. This is often known as a "peer review." People on the development committee or solicitation task force go over a list of names one by one. They talk about the prospects' interests, their likelihood to give to this project, and the appropriate amount to request. This can work in groups as well as in one-on-one meetings.

I love these sessions because they can be highly informative and incredibly helpful in gathering anecdotal information as well as hard data. They also help you discover the links and relationships between prospective donors and other people in the community.

Admittedly, not everyone is comfortable talking so frankly about his or her peers—especially in Christian circles. So I developed the *CPI Index*. The CPI Index is a form of research that attempts to "objectify" the information. Rather than talking with each other, participants score prospective donors on three criteria:

- Capacity to give,
- Philanthropic nature, and
- Interest in your ministry or the project.

Capacity: Do the potential donors have money they can donate to your ministry? If they don't, they won't be good fundraising prospects—no matter how nice they may be. Face it; you need cash to pay the bills and accomplish the mission God's calling you to. Even Mother Teresa was known to say, "Without money, there is no mission."

Philanthropic Nature: Are the individuals generous? If they don't give gifts to other charities, chances are high they won't contribute to yours.

Interest: Are the individuals interested in your cause? Bill Gates would have high scores in capacity and philanthropy, but without an interest in your ministry, he's not going to make a gift to you.

To conduct a CPI Index session, put your list of names on a spreadsheet with the three CPI columns. Then ask people to score the prospective donors in each area on a scale of 1 (being lowest) to 5 (being highest) in each of the categories. When they're done, add up the scores. You'll want to personally visit people with scores of 12 or higher and invite them to make a gift. Ask the group of peers who would be the best "door openers" to help you get in front of those people.

Prospect's Name	C (1-5)	P (1-5)	I (1-5)	Total	Notes
John Donor	4	3	4	11	Just sold his company

Don't toss out the names that scored lower! Be sure to look at the people who scored high C's and P's but only mediocre I's. Why? No matter how much you shop at a person's store or buy her products, you can't change a her capacity score. And you can't change her philanthropic nature— either she is generous or she is not. Generosity is usually something that comes from her family of origin or her faith tradition. But you *can* help her become more interested in your ministry! I'd recommend beginning to cultivate people with high C and P scores. You may find that many of them really aren't interested in your ministry. But you *will* find a few that will become incredibly committed if they're cultivated well. Cultivating well is the focus of our next chapter.

A note for people raising personal ministry support: Only large organizations will be using the tools in the "outsourcing research" paragraph. Don't be discouraged. Also, the peer index and CPI exercises are probably more easily done by larger ministries or colleges. They can be helpful in raising your own support, but don't get bogged down here. The reality is you are going to need to talk to everybody on your list. You'll have a much more personal approach to your fundraising that will be able to overcome a lot of analytical research. You will still be able to reach your goal!

TWO WARNINGS
Many of my clients, inside and outside the Church, get very uncomfortable with the information discovered in the research step. It is pretty amazing how much information is public and available. Remember, you're not the FBI. You're trying to help your ministry be an excellent steward of its limited resources. This kind of research helps significantly leverage the effectiveness of your fundraising.

The first warning is: *whatever you do, do not compromise your integrity.* I promise you that these forms of research are legitimate, ethical, and professional. Your integrity is worth more than any amount of funding you may raise for your ministry. Listen to the Holy Spirit and your conscience, and only go as far as you're comfortable. If you're getting uncomfortable with what you're finding, stop.

Usually, the largest barriers to our fundraising are *our own attitudes to wealth and money*. Before you give up on researching, make sure you're not stopping just because you glorify poverty. Ask God to heal your perspective on wealth before you put artificial limits on your ability to raise funds for your ministry.

A comforting result of research is that you feel more secure about your ask before you get in front of the donor. Research also ends up helping the donors as much as it helps you. If you found out they've written editorials against the things your ministry stands for, you won't waste their time asking them to support it!

The second warning is: *don't get stuck on this step*. Research feels great. You're visioning, dreaming, strategizing, finding potential funding, and feeling awesome about the calling God has given you. But research is just the beginning. The biggest potential danger in research is "paralysis by analysis." There is a very real risk that you will put off asking in an ongoing pursuit of finding out "just one more thing" about a prospect. You can do homework until the cows come home, but *nobody makes a gift until they're asked*.

I don't know how many boards I've sat on when the inevitable question arises: "Have you researched that? I know we're hemorrhaging financially, losing money hand-over-fist, but before we fix that by actually asking people for a gift, can we take a step back and do more research?" Research can be an easy way to chicken out of asking without looking like a coward. That kind of thinking will kill any fundraising effort. Sometimes, you just need to go for it and make the ask.

Now that we've established some of the advantages of research and some simple ways to do it, let's move on to our next part of getting R.E.A.L.: *engage.*

Chapter 2
Engage

"Computer dating is fine,
if you're a computer."
                    - Rita Mae Brown

"Relationships of trust depend
on our willingness to look not
only to our own interests, but
also the interests of others."
                    - Peter Farquharson

"Don't judge each day by the
harvest you reap but the seed
you plant."
                    - Robert Louis Stevenson

"Do two walk together unless
they have agreed to do so?"
                    - Amos 3:3

I'm amazed by how many ministry folks seem to think they can just jump into asking people for money. They go from not asking at all to assuming people will just give when petitioned.

What if asking for a gift were like getting married? A guy wants to get married, but he's scared to death of meeting people. So he stalls as long as he can. He stays inside and doesn't go on a single date. Then his parents start getting weird and talking about wanting grandchildren. The pressure keeps building. He begins to believe he really *needs* to get married! So he runs out of his house down to the nearest bar, plops down on a stool, and asks the first woman he sees if she'll marry him! Crazy, isn't it? What's even crazier is that he gets upset when she slaps him and says "No!"

That scenario can play out in fundraising. Funding is needed, but the reluctant fundraiser avoids asking people for money. Oh, he might hint at it or talk in general terms but never make a *direct ask*. He couches suggestions in between "praise reports" and "prayer requests." He thinks that people will somehow figure out that "support our work" means to give cash. Preferably monthly.

So he avoids asking but continues wanting the funding. At some point, his ministry gets into a financial crisis, and he is forced to ask people directly for money. Then he panics and sends lots of letters to a general (and perhaps inappropriate) list of people who are suspected prospects rather than true prospects. Maybe he photocopies a sheet and inserts it with the church bulletin. Or he may spam people's Facebook newsfeeds and email inboxes.

Then he gets angry when nobody gives!

In both dating and fundraising, *you need to get to know people before you ask* them to make a commitment. You need to *engage* them in the process.

Engaging people involves being genuinely interested in them, not just in their checkbook (or your perception of their checkbook— some folks look wealthy but are simply "broke at a higher level").

Some of the ways you can engage people are to:

- Take them out to lunch (and pick up the tab).
- Ask them about their story. If they're Christians, ask them about their faith.
- Visit them when you're traveling in their area.
- Send them articles you think might interest them.

The point is to take note of what interests people and what doesn't. You are doing them the courtesy *of trying to find something in your cause that relates to their interests*. Asking someone to make a substantial gift to a cause they don't care about is pointless!

As it is in dating, "engaging" in fundraising is a two-way process. Both parties get to know the other party. I often let people know my interests outside of work. It is *amazing* to see how comments like this help people to open up. I think they start to view me as a real person, not just someone trying to reach into their wallet.

Don't talk incessantly about your needs. Study after study shows that people give to winning causes, not to needs! I think many in the nonprofit world often look like Bill Murray's character in the movie "What About Bob?". He is constantly whining to his psychiatrist, "I want. I want. I want. I need. I need. I need!" *Donors aren't motivated by need.*

Instead, let people know the cool things your ministry is doing. This helps them see that their gift will be well used. Show them how their gift can play a real part in expanding God's Kingdom.

A few years ago, I met with a prospective funder to see if his company's priorities would match with one of our events. Rather than rattling through a prepared pitch about the event, I spent a good portion of the time practically bragging about some innovative things our hospital was doing. (We were one of the first hospitals in the entire U.S. to disclose our clinical outcomes voluntarily on the web. Having it right on our website allowed patients to make an informed decision about whether or not they should get cared for by us. That took guts!)

Letting them know the exceptional quality of our advanced service prepared the groundwork for understanding that their giving would contribute to a winning cause. The funder found that incredibly compelling and became a sponsor.

The "engage" step is even more important than researching. No one raises large amounts of money from behind a desk. As fundraising guru Si Seymour used to say, "You can't milk a cow with a letter."

Fundraising is all about relationships. So get out there and meet your prospects!

Getting to Know You

It can be hard to figure out how to start these conversations. The best way I've found is to remember why you got involved. In ministry, it's as much about your passion for Jesus as it is about the outcomes He's helping you make. Some donor prospects will get excited about your faith. Others will be more interested in the people you are feeding, the students hearing the Gospel, or the land being stewarded in a more godly manner. So be sure to think about both your faith story *and* the reason why you're expressing it in this ministry. What excites *you* most about your work? People connect with passion. The best place to begin that process is by starting with your passion. If you're having a hard time reconnecting emotionally with that, take some time to pray. Ask God to rekindle the fire. Spend some time where the mission is happening. Being on the frontlines has a way of refocusing us and recommitting us.

Then, when you're interacting with people, start by exploring the interests of the other person. I love asking questions like:

- So what do you do when you're not eating lunch at this restaurant [or whatever activity you're both doing at the time]?
- How long have you been doing that?
- Really? How did you get started?

Bob Burg's book *Endless Referrals* is filled with great questions like this. Fortunately, I love hearing people's stories. I find people generally like telling their stories if they see you're genuinely interested. In our world, people are usually too busy or distracted to care. When you give someone permission to tell their story, you are giving them a tremendous gift.

Another way to get to know the other person is to look around their room or office. What awards and pictures are adorning the walls? Do they belong to any service clubs?

Personally, I love books, so I always look at bookshelves. Once I was in a home in California that had two small elegant wood and bronze plaques on the bookshelves. It turns out they were two patents for freeze-dried coffee! This got me excited! Beyond thinking about the potential royalties or licensing income the prospect might be making, I started thinking about all the challenges involved in earning a patent. He must have committed years of his life to this project. Those thoughts triggered questions that resulted in a fascinating conversation. (While he still became a donor, it turns out there were no royalties. Since he created this while he was an employee, the company owned all rights to the invention. Both of us commiserated about that!)

Getting Behind the Scenes

In his book *The Anatomy of Buzz*, Emmanuel Rosen talks about a third tool for engaging: "behind-the-scenes" experiences. Rosen says we all love to feel like we're getting a behind-the-scenes look at something. Even if we know it's not *really* behind-the-scenes, we still feel special if it's an "insider's" tour.

I fondly remember Walt Disney World's "Keys to the Kingdom" tour I took in 1998. For approximately five hours, we walked "backstage" and saw all sorts of "secrets" of the kingdom. We knew that we weren't actually seeing all the secrets, but it sure felt like we were. The tour certainly exceeded my expectations. For a person like me, that helped increase my enjoyment of the park on each subsequent visit. More importantly, I keep referring to that tour (even more than a decade later).

The same is true for your donors. If you're working with an international development ministry, you already know about the power of hosting tours of projects in the developing world. These behind-the-scenes activities help donors buy-in even more to a cause they already like.

You don't need to be doing international work to give your donors and donor prospects an inside look. Here are a few ways to possibly include your donor prospects in a behind-the-scenes activity:

Facility and Construction Tours

If your ministry facilities are expanding, you could host a gathering at your construction site and have the general contractor or architect speak. Make sure people are wearing hard hats. There is *magic* in the people wearing hard hats!

But even if there isn't construction, getting to the facility is moving to most prospects. Seeing the food kitchen in action, eating lunch in the cafeteria surrounded by students, or seeing the clinic are all great ways to connect prospects with the reality of your mission. As Christians, this shouldn't surprise us. Jesus needed to be born physically as a human for us to finally get into right relationship with God. Why wouldn't physical location be similarly necessary for prospects to relate to your ministry?

Monthly Q&A's with your Ministry Leader

You might hold a relaxed Q & A with yourself, your director, Board President, etc. This could be hosted in person (sort of a monthly tea) or virtually by using a tool like Google Hangouts on Air. The beauty of a Hangout on Air is that the Hangout is recorded and always available on your YouTube channel. These videos not only share your mission and vision expressed as answers to questions you're receiving, but they can also show the transparency in your ministry style. You have nothing to hide. This form of transparency is a simple way to build deep trust with donors and prospects.

Mission Moments

You could consider giving a tour of something you don't usually showcase. Fundraising events guru Shanon Doolittle talks about sharing "mission moments." You can share moments from regular activities that are central to your mission. One nonprofit she worked with rehabilitated animals. Once the animals were healthy, they were released back into the wild. She convinced the organization that the releasing event was perfect for donors and prospects. And she was right! People *loved* being invited to these.

Just because you're familiar with a task doesn't mean it isn't special. Perhaps you could take donors on a drive as you pray over potential locations for your church plant. If you regularly give presentations, bring some donors or prospects along. Be sure to let them see what God is doing in the ministry.

What I love most about the behind-the-scenes aspect of engaging is that it often can be done with little or no expense. Since it's behind-the-scenes, donors and prospects don't expect it to be as glitzy or as polished as a regular event would be! The unsophisticated nature of the event actually adds to its appeal.

While working at a Christian school, I gave a "behind-the-scenes" feel to class representatives by creating a monthly one-page/two-sided newsletter called "Rep Rap." Using a simple desktop publishing program, I developed this newsletter, photocopied them, and sent them out as self-mailers. The desktop publishing and photocopying were specifically intended to be non-flashy and create an informal feel. I wanted class reps to feel like they were getting something hot-off-the-press so they would know they were in an inner-circle. A glossy, four-color publication wouldn't have done that.

If you can't bring the donors to these "behind-the-scenes" events, bring the events to the donors! Social media is great for this. One Christian recording artist showcases his week in the Nashville studio on his Facebook page. He includes pictures, videos, and responses to questions people are sending him. You could tweet your way through a legislative or city council budget meeting, or whatever meeting your ministry may be attending. You could also take quick "behind the scenes" videos and upload them to YouTube. Then the videos can be posted on your webpage, blogs, and all sorts of other sites.

Don't Get Stuck Here

As fun as engaging is, don't get stuck in this step either. No prospect has ever made a significant gift just because you were friendly and engaging. You may have heard of "friendraising" and seen Christians say "friendraising" is more important than fundraising. Rubbish. I'm convinced that donors aren't desperately looking for more friends. And while donors may become your friends, friendship isn't the goal. Fundraising is. People need to be directly asked to give. And they'll get a bit frustrated with you if you don't get around to it.

So once you do your *research* and *engage* the prospective donor, it's time for the moment of truth: *asking for money*!

Chapter 3
Ask

"Much is required from those to whom much is given."
- Jesus, Luke 12:48

"To keep a lamp burning we have to keep putting oil in it."
- Mother Teresa

"No one has ever become poor by giving."
- Anne Frank

"God gives, but man must open his hand."
- German Proverb

"When courage, genius, and generosity hold hands, all things are possible."
- Unknown

"The greatest use of a life is to
spend it on something that will
outlast it."

- William James

"There are two ways of
spreading light: to be the candle
or the mirror that reflects it."

- Edith Wharton

Do you know the #1 reason people give money to nonprofits? *They are asked.*

If you only could do one step of the Get R.E.A.L. process, and raising money is your goal, "ask" is the step you'd want to choose.

Which do you think is easier: Walking up to a stranger and asking her to give you money? Or calling a person you've gotten to know and asking her to invest in a mission that interests her?

Do you see that after doing your *research* and *engaging* the donor, asking is a breeze? The first two steps help you determine the people who won't be interested. This lets you spend your asking time on the people who *will* be interested.

Before you start asking individuals for their gifts, be sure you've made *your* gift first. People can tell if you're committed or not. You give your blood, sweat, and tears. You've committed your life and livelihood; but unfortunately, those aspects aren't as easy to measure as money. You don't need to be making the same leadership gifts as those you're asking. But I seriously think you should consider giving a minimum of $1000 a year—that's about $84 a month. If you're asking a donor to consider doubling her giving, you should ask yourself to consider doubling *your* giving first. (And if you're asking people to give out of their tithe, you need to be tithing, too.)

It's so much easier to ask people to *join* you in supporting the project than it is to ask them to give money to something you're not investing in personally. Plus, people are pretty smart. They intuitively know if you've given money, and they are far less likely to give if you haven't.

A word about George Mueller

One of the biggest objections I get from people in ministry is about asking directly. They ask, "Shouldn't we only tell God—like George Mueller?"

Then I ask, "Well, how is that working for you?"

It's usually not. George Mueller was an amazing saint. But as ministry fundraising expert Scott Morton says in his book *Funding Your Ministry*, Mueller's approach had a lot to do with his faith journey. As a young man, Mueller was manipulative and deceitful. In fact, his father had to lay an elaborate trap to catch him stealing money.

Something about the "only telling God" was very important in his journey with Jesus. It shaped his character. But his style is not a blueprint for everyone. Not everyone has the same avarice Mueller did before meeting Jesus.

Morton also points out that Mueller's "informing" others was an indirect ask. That is a form of asking that is sometimes called a "soft ask." It's not one I advise, but it is on the "asking" spectrum. As he told about his financial prayers being answered, he was making people aware of the very real financial needs of his ministry.

I agree with Morton that for most people, relying on the "Mueller Method" is more of a cop-out than a leap of faith. Fundraisers can be so afraid of rejection that they don't risk asking. Remember that the Biblical approach to funding is much broader than just one man's experience.

Most ministries I know of grow in faith by putting themselves out there and asking directly. This approach takes immense amounts of courage, conviction, and prayer just like the example of Nehemiah when he asked for financing to rebuild the walls of Jerusalem. The Kingdom of God is not expanded by cowardice.

I'd recommend erring on the side of asking. If God only wants you talking to Him, He'll make it known.

Remember the ministry aspect of asking, too. People need to give. God is clear in His Word that His followers are expected to be generous. So their giving is a necessary aspect of their own faith journey. Sometimes they don't realize their need until they receive a well-communicated ask.

Setting up an Appointment

If you're setting up an appointment for a solicitation, please be honest about it. When I made my first few asks for a Christian college, I set up the appointments without letting people know I was going to ask them for money. I'd often use the approach: "I'm going to be in your area—could I just drop in?" And I always felt icky. I spent my entire time with them trying to manipulate the conversation around to something that would let me make the ask. I felt like I pulled a "bait-and-switch." I'd said I just wanted to meet for coffee, but I had an ulterior motive. So now when I'm setting up an appointment to ask for money I always make sure the donor prospect knows that I'm expecting to ask her to invest in my cause.

You might say something as simple as, "I'm going to be in the area, and I would love to get together with you to talk about a big project we're working on." You could even say something as specific as, "While we're together, I'd really like to talk about your involvement in our ministry." If you've developed a relationship with her this far, she knows you need to invite people to invest in your work. A solicitation isn't going to surprise her. This shows her the courtesy of letting her know your agenda in advance. It also makes your meetings so much easier. If you start to ramble during your appointment, she'll help get you back on track by saying something like, "This is all nice, but didn't you ask me here to talk about your ministry?"

When setting up an appointment, I like asking if her "calendar would allow" us to meet at such-and-such a time. "I'll be traveling in your area next week. Would your calendar allow us to get together Tuesday morning or Wednesday afternoon?" I find that wording makes the process of setting up an appointment less confrontational. Some would argue against using this phrase saying it lets the prospective donor off the hook by not compelling her to take personal responsibility for her time. But my goal isn't to be her life coach. My goal is to raise money. Asking if her calendar will allow us to get together feels less confrontational to me.

Making the Ask

Sometimes clients ask me what qualifies as an "ask." For me, getting together with a donor doesn't qualify as an ask unless I've asked for a gift of a specific dollar amount. A vague question doesn't do it. For example, "Would you consider supporting us?" The donor has no idea what you're requesting. She may think you mean praying for you, or "liking" your Facebook page, or giving you a pat on the back. She may even think you mean a one-time $25 gift when you're really hoping for $150 each month.

To be clear, try using phrases like:

- Would you consider giving $xxx each month?
- I'd like to ask you to consider giving $10,000 to our project.
- I was thinking about asking you to give $25,000 to the fund over the next 3 years. Is that a possibility?

I'd normally encourage you to ask for the total gift at this point, not breaking it down into payments. It's good for her to have a "deer in the headlights' look—to realize that you are asking her to prioritize the ministry in their philanthropic giving. Telling her about payment options is great after she has considered the total gift.

However, when you are raising personal support, monthly options can work. You could try:

- I'd like to invite you to join our monthly supporters at the $xxx level.

- We're focusing on building our support team at the $150/month level. Would you consider being part of that?

- We are only 10 donors away from filling up the needed $100/month donors on our support team. Could we invite you to join?

To be completely clear in terms of what you're asking for is critical. If you are scared while you're in front of the prospect, *just be honest with her.* Honesty and integrity are two of the most powerful fundraising tools in your tool belt. You could say, "I'm really sorry, but I'm really nervous. I love [whatever your ministry does], but I'm not used to asking people to give to it. But [the kids, etc.] mean so much to me, I'm willing to get outside of my comfort zone. So, would you consider … "

When you admit you are nervous, the prospect will completely identify. She doesn't like asking either! Your confession will clear the air. She'll realize the tension isn't about her at all. Often she'll even try to cheer you on in asking her.

Stop talking
Once the ask is out clearly and succinctly, **SHUT UP!**

Make the ask, and *be quiet.* This is so hard! As long as you're talking, you feel like you're in control. But if you keep talking now, you'll talk the donor right out of giving. Sales trainers say, "he who speaks first loses." It's not about winning and losing here; it's about treating the donor with respect. You've just asked her to do something she's probably never considered doing for your ministry. She needs time to process. She'll be thinking about how much money is in her account, the amount that she can afford to give to your cause, and how she'll explain this to her spouse. Some people are slow processors; some people are fast.

She'll let you know when she's done processing by being the first to speak.

Once she speaks, you can tell her that $1000 a year is around $84 per month. This is when to let her know that gifts can be made by credit card. After she speaks is the appropriate time to mention whatever else you wanted to say while you were shutting up. Speaking before she does may short-circuit the important thinking process she's going through and cause her to simply say, "No."

Finding an Outlet

I'm a firm believer in keeping things simple. Simplicity has a beauty of its own. Unfortunately, it's really easy to overcomplicate teaching about "making the ask." When it comes right down to it, *asking for money is simply story telling.*

1. You figure out who is most likely to respond well to your story.

2. You give those people the opportunity to tell *their* story.

3. You show them points of intersection with their story and your story.

4. You show them how their support can impact your ministry and the greater Kingdom.

5. You ask if they'd consider investing in one of those points of intersection.

6. Then you go and tell that story to the next prospect.

You'll find that solicitations can be some of the most fun experiences of your life!

Remember my analogy of the fundraiser looking for the connection between the donor's electrical cord and the nonprofit's outlet? *Asking is inviting her to plug into your ministry.* That's where the power is released! Remember the things that get her excited. If she doesn't care about "a hand up and not a handout," or "souls saved," or "missiological theory," don't talk about those aspects of your mission—even if they're normally a big part of your prepared solicitation speech! Focus on what interests her and ask her to invest in *that.*

Concentrating on the donor's interests isn't demonstrating a lack of integrity. Your ministry or nonprofit is like a jewel. Jewels have many facets. Your job is to turn the jewel so the donor sees the facet that makes the biggest connection with her. You are still holding the entire jewel, but you don't need to get her to understand everything about it. Your job is to get her to invest in the ministry. You can trust that she'll come to appreciate the other facets as she continues to invest.

Sometimes what is important to her is not about the ministry at all. When I was an alumni director for a Christian boarding school many years ago, I experienced one of the oddest alumni meetings I've ever had. After tossing back a couple of martinis (him, not me), an alumnus said, "Aww [expletive]! I forgot my checkbook.

You *never* see the alumni director without your checkbook!"

It was as though he had been given a script before our meeting! I honestly hadn't come to ask him for money this time. But he knew that nonprofits need philanthropic support and that relationships with donors are a kind of dance.

Given an invitation like that, and having listened to him talk about his habit of buying a $1,500 suit each quarter, I decided to ask for a gift. But rather than a gift in line with his regular annual giving, I asked if he'd consider giving up his next suit and give that money to the school instead. It didn't work, but it definitely got his attention. He was impressed that I actually listened to him and asked him something related to his life.

Using Props

One of my primary goals is to help you feel comfortable enough to ask people to consider investing in your ministry—especially if you're not a paid professional development officer. Passionate volunteers make organizations a special part of the community.

Even with the best preparation, it can sometimes be nerve-wracking to ask for a gift. Have you ever set up a solicitation appointment and gone to the meeting only to chicken out of asking? You are not alone. You may try to justify it by saying the time "wasn't right," but you leave feeling like you've really let your cause down. Worse, the donor leaves confused because you'd set up the appointment specifically to ask her for money, but you never got to that point in the conversation.

Using props can be a great way to help you avoid chickening out. There's power in putting a piece of paper on the desk or showing a video on a tablet. All of a sudden, the solicitation is no longer "you against her." Instead, you're both focusing on the same thing. It's as though you've moved over to her side of the table and formed an initial partnership.

One of the easiest props to use is **the gift grid** you created during the research stage. (If you didn't do it then, try it now. You can create one for free by going to http://www.GiftRangeCalculator. com/.) This is one of my favorite props. It shows the prospect that you're not asking her to fund the entire budget. It also demonstrates that you believe so strongly in your mission that you've taken the time to create a professional strategy.

Saying the actual dollar amount may be an obstacle for you. Instead of asking for $25,000, you can simply point to that section of the gift grid and ask, "Would you consider giving at this level?" The prospect has a very specific idea of what you're requesting. There's no ambiguity. Another advantage is that she can see the entire range of gifts. She just may say, "No, not at that level. I'd like to give at this (higher) level." That has happened!

This grid can also become a great prospecting tool. Whether the person says "yes" or "no" to your solicitation, you should always ask if there is anyone she would recommend you approach about giving at that level. She may not be able to think of anyone, but at least you've asked. If she *does* think of someone, you've significantly decreased your research time on that new person. With permission, you can call the new prospect and say, "I was just talking about this campaign with Jane, and she suggested I show it to you, too. I'll be in your area this week. Would your calendar allow us to meet this Thursday or next Tuesday?"

Another prop that I believe just might be the most effective is **a picture of the completed project**. These are often called renderings or perspectives. Get an artist to paint a picture of what the room will look like when it's finished. Or the kids being fed. Or people using the land that's been conserved. If you are just getting started, look to see if this sort of project has been completed somewhere else. You might be able to get the picture of what it looks like to show at your meeting.

Not only will the picture communicate what you intend to do, but it also shows the prospect that such a project can be completed successfully. Don't underestimate the power of this. Every donor wants to know she's investing in a winning cause or contributing to a project that actually will be accomplished. A picture can help the donor visualize success and reassure her that you'll see this project through to completion.

Here's a lesson from experience: If you're using architectural blueprints with the floor plans of a building project, highlight the existing building. A few years back, I used floor plans to help me tell the story of expanding a nursing home. I told donors that the expansion almost doubled our floor space. But I only had floor plans that showed what the facility would look like in the future! The #1 question I got when I gave a tour was "What exists right now?"

These floor plans would have been far more impressive if the original footprint were somehow marked on them. Then the prospects could see what the old space was and how this new space would be so much better. They wouldn't have to take my word about the doubling of floor space; the evidence would be directly in front of them. Many of our prospects had been visiting the nursing home for the last 30 years. They were familiar with the building as it had been for that time, but they could not visualize what it was going to become. Having the original footprint would have made it easier for them to orient themselves so they could appreciate the project.

One important note: *don't use the prop as a substitute for asking.* A danger with great props is that you'll succumb to the temptation of just popping them in the mail with a personal note. I call this the "Field of Dreams Fallacy," and I discuss it in Chapter 5 as Fundraising Faux Pas #1. Don't give in to the temptation! Make sure to P.Y.I.T.S.—*put yourself in their shoes*. Would you make a significant gift if you received a gift grid in the mail? Probably not. *So don't risk it with your prospect. Your cause is too important.* Get on the phone, set up the solicitation appointment, and bring the prop with you. You'll be glad you did!

Tangibilitize Your Ask

When I give seminars, I encourage people to tangibilitize their ask. You won't find "tangibilitize" in the dictionary, but you will find it in practice all around you. Look at any piece of direct mail you receive that's trying to get you to spend money. The good ones will break down "what you'll get" for the cost of the investment. These concrete examples help make the offer tangible. Tangibilitizing is all about taking someone's abstract gift of money and making it real.

Once again, *put yourself in the shoes of the donor*. Someone's just asked you to give $1,000 to her project. She's done an excellent job presenting her case, and you're convinced her ministry is doing incredible work. But give $1,000 from your personal account? Where will that come from?! And how would your $1,000 *really* help them? She needs to tell you clearly what your gift would help them do.

In fundraising for your ministry, it's up to *you* to tell your donor. Ask yourself, *what would $1000 do for your ministry?*

- How much more outreach could you do in the community?
- What kind of children's programs would $1000 allow you to add?
- What technology would you add?

- How much of a day would that help fund? (Think of radio stations' "Day Sponsors.")
- How many books or films could you buy?

Anything can be fair game. Do what you can to make an investment of money become tangible. Make it something the donor can get her heart behind.

Heifer International tangibilitizes extraordinarily well. Go to www.heifer.org and take a look at their gift catalog. A while ago, they represented it like this:

*Need help? Have a question? Please email us at info@heifer.org or call us at **1-800-422-0474**.*

The prices in this catalog represent the complete livestock gift of a quality animal, technical assistance and training. Each purchase is symbolic and represents a contribution to the entire mission of Heifer International. Donations will be used where needed most to help struggling people.

Different animals represented the gift ranges:
- $500 as a gift of a heifer
- $120 as a gift of a pig
- $60 as a trio of rabbits
- $20 as a gift of chickens
- $5000 as a gift of an ark!

Every gift in the catalog describes the many ways people will benefit. For example, chickens help Mrs. Ndagurwa
- scratch up and fertilize her vegetable garden
- give her 200+ eggs per year, adding protein to her family's diet and
- provide income (by selling some eggs) to help her market her vegetables.

Can you see how much more compelling a "gift of chickens" can be than simply asking for $20?

What I love about Heifer.org is the clear statement right under the image of the animals:

> The prices in this catalog represent the complete livestock gift of a quality animal, technical assistance and training. Each purchase is symbolic and represents a contribution to the entire mission of Heifer International. Donations will be used where needed most to help struggling people.

With a statement like that, you know exactly what you're giving to and how the gift will be used.

How can you tangibilitize your ministry? Why not stop right now and find the answers to these questions:

- How many people will be served by a gift of $1,000?

- How many days (or hours) of programming will a gift of $5,000 fund?

- How many people will be served? How many visits will that generate to local businesses?

- How many jobs created? Students assisted?

As you make your solicitation tangible, do not overwhelm the other person with too many options (Refer to Chapter 5 about Fundraising Faux Pas #3 "The Cheez-It Treatment"). It's important to have lots of ways to tangibilitize your ask, but only use the one or two that will best fit with the other person's interests.

Watch Your Phrasing

Finally, when you're asking for money, you'd do well to take the advice of Mayor Shin in the musical "The Music Man." One of his favorite warnings to people is "Watch your phraseology!"

At some point you'll probably say the wrong words to a donor and become really embarrassed. Just read the story I call "Mrs. McTat's House of Cat's" in the *Fundraising Faux Pas* chapter.

Practice will increase your odds of saying the right thing. I recommend you practice the ask by talking to your steering wheel. While you're out doing errands, say the ask over. Try out the different phrasing. See what wording flows more naturally for you.

It's important for you to make the ask smoothly. If you hesitate or stumble over wording, the donor will see that and tense up. She won't know what the tension is about and may decide it's a red flag for her not to invest in you.

In my experience, and that of my clients, one of the best phrases to practice is:

> *"I'd like to ask you to consider a gift of $25,000 to the campaign."*

This phrase will be one of the most valuable tools in your fundraising tool belt. Stop for a minute right now and say it out loud. Could you say the "$25,000" dollar amount naturally? If not, keep practicing until it rolls off your tongue.

Since you've already made your own gift, you could easily change that phrase to be:

> *"Would you consider joining me in making a gift of $25,000 to the campaign?"*

or

> *"Would you consider joining me in supporting the campaign with a gift of $25,000?"*

Dealing with Objections

Generally what a donor says when she's done processing internally isn't a straight "yes" or "no." It's usually an obstacle stated as an objection. I used to hate objections because I was afraid I wouldn't have all the right answers. So, I naively hoped they simply wouldn't have any objections. But that just isn't realistic. I've come to realize that objections are good. In most cases, objections are an indication from the prospect that she is interested in making a donation. *Objections are just obstacles in her way of making that gift.* So the next step in the solicitation is working together to overcome those obstacles. It turns out that objections are actually continuing the solicitation conversation.

It's always good to be prepared with an affirmative response to an objection. When you ask a person for money, you're putting her on the spot. You're asking her to do something that she hasn't done up to this point. In a way, you've put yourself at odds with the prospect. Your role from this point on is to get yourself back to the same side of the table.

Affirming an objection with a simple phrase like: "I can appreciate that ... " helps you do just that. You can even say, "I can appreciate that ... " and leave it hanging. Let the silence fill the air and watch what happens. The other person will often fill the silence by reminding herself why giving the gift is so important. A verbal processor needs to hear herself explain why it is important for her to give a gift. It's hard to be quiet at times like this, but it's crucial!

The great thing about the phrase "I can appreciate that" is that no matter what she says, you really can appreciate it—even if you don't agree. Chances are, you'd feel the same way if you were in her shoes. Affirming her objection is not the same as falling into the trap of *accepting* her excuse. Your job is still to raise funds. Just saying an affirming phrase can help her feel less defensive.

Another effective way to overcome objections is the technique known as "Feel. Felt. Found." "I know how you *feel*. I *felt* the same way. Here's what I *found* ... " This is particularly helpful if you did feel the same way as the prospect. But be careful. "Feel. Felt. Found." is a technique that many people learn. It can begin to sound like a trite formula when it's used too frequently.

A Simple Exercise To Identify Objections *Before They Happen*
Sales guru Zig Ziglar claims that for any given experience like this, there are *generally only four or five objections*. I've worked with nonprofits and ministries around the world and found this to be true. (Although some university teams came up with 10 or 11 objections! Over-achievers!)

If it's true that there are a set number of objections, why not figure them out in advance? Pull your team together and have a brainstorming session. This can be with your staff, your board, or with other people raising support. Put all the objections to making a gift to your cause (real, imagined, and off-the-wall) on sticky notes. Limit it to one objection per note. Then get all the notes up on the wall.

When everyone is done, start grouping the notes into similar categories: the "my kids are in college" category, the "this has been a hard year for my business" category, the "we give to our church" category, and so on. You'll probably find that all of the objections (with some teams will come up with hundreds of phrases) fit into four or five categories.

Now that you have identified the most common objections, brainstorm answers! As the group works together coming up with answers to these objections, the confidence each answer creates becomes infectious. Rather than memorizing canned phrases, your team can put their own words and experiences into overcoming objections.

As your team develops phrasing for overcoming peoples' objections, be on the lookout for stories of people in similar situations who are giving anyway. One person's story can conquer a truck full of statistics. And once you've created these phrases and stories, make sure to work them into your "engage" activities and your "ask" presentations.

You'll be overcoming the objections before they even come up!

A Word on Tithing

Some Christians will say they won't support your ministry because they are already tithing to their church. While this sounds holy and good, don't be afraid to push. Statistics in the USA show that even people who say they "tithe" are only giving 2% of their income, not the 10% that is the definition of tithing. More importantly, **nowhere in Scripture is tithing seen as the end of giving**. Scripture focuses more on generosity and giving willingly. Tithing is presented as merely a first step to a generous life.

In my own fundraising, I thank a person who says she tithes. I wish all Christians tithed! I might even say I wasn't asking her to consider changing her tithe. But I ask her again to consider including the ministry in her "stewardship giving." This lets her know I see her as a generous person. And it gets the conversation back on supporting my ministry.

More On Overcoming Objections

Another effective method for working with objections comes from Jeffrey Fox's book *How to be a Rainmaker*. Fox recommends turning objections into objectives. If the prospect's *objection is*, "I can't possibly give to the campaign with both of my kids in college." You can answer, "So our *objective* is to figure out how to help you make the gift you want to the campaign while spreading out the pledge payments to make tuition payments easy. Is that it?"

By turning the objection into an objective, you've put yourself back on the same side of the table as the other person. Now you are working together to figure out how to help the donor make the gift. You've taken a possibly challenging problem and made solving it a team effort.

As we wrap up this section, it's important to remember that **you don't have to answer every objection**. I was once in a solicitation with an influential community member. I'd asked him to *triple* his gift to our organization. He had more questions/objections than

I'd ever encountered in an ask! I felt like I was on an objection treadmill— and I was in danger of falling off.

At one point, I gathered up the courage to ask him, *"If I am able to answer this, is this the only thing standing in the way of you making a gift?"*

This was so helpful. He said it wasn't—he had a bigger objection. So we skipped over this one and went on to the real issue.

Unfortunately, his "big" question was one I thought I'd already answered a couple of times during this visit! I knew if I hadn't been able to answer it yet, I wouldn't be able to this time. I tried one last ditch effort. Feeling a sinking desperation, I asked, *"If I can't answer this to your satisfaction, would this stop you from making the gift?"*

As he thought about this, I really began to feel that I might have pushed him too far. This was as hard as the "shutting up" after the initial solicitation. But I endured the silence and let him process my question. After some time, he said, "You know? No. Even if you can't answer this in a way I understand, I still want to make the gift to help you guys."

And like that, he tripled his annual gift! *You really don't have to answer every objection.*

So you've researched, engaged, and asked. After having been through all these steps, you hope they'll make a gift at some level. But sometimes, even with all the great work you've done, they decide not to give. That brings us to the final phase of the Get R.E.A.L. process: *love.*

Donna Wilson has been coaching and training InterVarsity staffers in raising their own support for over 40 years. I've asked her to share her insights into some of the changes she's seen in fundraising in an increasingly pluralistic society.

MINISTRY FUNDRAISING IN A NON-MAJORITY CULTURAL CONTEXT

By Donna Wilson
Senior Consultant & National MPD Coach
InterVarsity Christian Fellowship/USA

Culture influences almost every part of our lives—how we communicate as well as our customs, practices, behavior, beliefs, relationships, and more. So when we engage in fundraising it's important to remember that it too has evolved within a particular cultural context. Many fundraising practices developed in North America years ago when economic resources were primarily managed by "majority culture," which was basically White males. The principles of fundraising that evolved were therefore designed to engage majority culture male donors. When a ministry worker from a non-majority culture is fundraising, however, he or she will often experience cultural dissonance with standard fundraising techniques. Furthermore, non-majority culture donors may feel disrespected or even offended when they are asked to give in a way that is inappropriate in their culture.

Donors from communities of color are extremely generous, typically giving much larger percentages of their incomes than their counterparts of majority culture. However, giving in communities of color usually looks very different. These cultures are more communal by nature. While White culture is proud of its individualism and self-sufficiency, most communities of color see interdependence as an important value. Giving is often within the family unit, with family being defined much more broadly than in White culture. Giving frequently involves "in-kind" gifts such as free food, housing, or childcare. This tradition of caring for one another means that most giving is done in the context of a group, with needs of the larger community in mind— not a single person's needs. In this cultural context elders and community leaders will be critical people to involve in your presentation. It is also very important to show how the ministry outcomes will benefit the community as a whole.

Communities of color also tend to be more hierarchical and paternalistic than majority culture. Whereas White culture enjoys informality and avoids behavior that would position one person above another, communities of color see age, gender, and social status as realities to be acknowledged and honored. For instance, it might be inappropriate for a young ministry worker to approach an older member of the community and ask directly for funds, as that kind of familiarity could appear disrespectful. In those cases, engaging a third party as an advocate may be much more culturally appropriate.

Differing views of time is another piece to take into consideration when fundraising cross-culturally. Current majority culture tends to see time as "fixed" and therefore a key driver of activities. Because efficient use of time is a high value, a good fundraising appointment may need to be very focused and succinct. However, many non-majority cultures view time as "fluid" and see expectations about relationships as the real driver of activities. In fluid-time cultures, fundraising appointments often need to include a lot of conversation about family, life, and other issues that may not seem directly related to the reason for the appointment. Sharing hospitality in an unhurried way is an important piece of the "engage" step.

Another extremely important element of culture relates to communication styles. White culture and many Black cultures tend to be direct in their communication style. People are clear about what they are thinking and what they are asking for. However, in honor/shame cultures such as Asian or Latino communities, communication tends to be indirect so that the initiator does not experience a "loss of face" if their request is turned down. Indirect communication leaves space for dignity; since the request is not overt, a response can simply be avoided if it is not positive. In the fundraising context this means that the level of directness employed by a fundraiser when doing an "ask" has a whole range of possibilities depending on cultural context, social status, and level of familiarity. Sometimes simply making the need known but not directly asking a prospect to give is an appropriate kind of "indirect ask" that will communicate clearly to someone from an indirect culture. Other times a softer "direct ask" might be made through a letter or email, thus avoiding the face-to-face relational pressures.

For a fundraiser it's important to first get to know the culture of the person you are hoping to invite into partnership so that you can understand how the fundraising process needs to be nuanced to fit that culture. In addition, consider how you might need to overcome some of your own cultural discomfort in order to relate appropriately to your potential donor. For instance, if you come from an Asian context, a direct ask may feel very uncomfortable; however, if you are relating to someone from a direct cultural context, he or she probably will not understand your ask if it is done in an indirect way. As the fundraiser you will need to adapt to the culture of your potential donor, the donor does not need to adapt to your culture.

If you have limited cross-cultural experience, you will need to listen, observe, and ask lots of questions. Be careful not to judge, but be open to new experiences. You may want to engage in some cross-cultural training or ask a friend from the culture you are entering to be a "cultural guide," helping you understand the cultural nuances.

Being sensitive to cultural contexts is an important part of asking "without fear."

Chapter 4
Love

"Silent gratitude isn't much use
to anyone."
                - Gladys Browyn Stern

"And now these three remain:
faith, hope and love. But the
greatest of these is love."
                - 1 Corinthians 13:13

"He that gives should never
remember, he that receives
should never forget."
                - Talmud

"The deepest principle in
human nature is the craving to
be appreciated."
                - William James

"Feeling gratitude and not
expressing it is like wrapping a
gift and not giving it."
                - Unknown

"Be thankful for what you have;
you'll end up having more. If you
concentrate on what you don't have,
you will never, ever have enough."
                        - Oprah Winfrey

"Appreciation can make a day—even
change a life. Your willingness
to put it into words is all that is
necessary."
                    - Margaret Cousins

"The meeting of two personalities
is like the contact of two chemical
substances: if there is any reaction,
both are transformed."
                            - Carl Jung

Congratulations! You've done your research, engaged your prospect, asked him for money, and answered his objections.

So, what do you do now?

It is tremendous if he says, "Yes! I am thrilled to give you a gift at the level you asked for." This is when your stewardship system kicks in. You're able to make your first action in the "Love" step: you get to say, "Thank you." Say it verbally, right there. Then make sure to send a thank-you note later.

Of course, there is a possibility that if he says "yes" too easily, your ask was too low. If you think that's the case, you could try a strategy I learned from a Christian Stewardship Association session. The teacher told the audience, "As calmly and smoothly as possible try asking, 'A year, for the next three years?'" I've used this technique for years, and it works!

In most cases, however, you'll be better off saying thank you. This isn't the only time you'll be communicating with him. Your goal is to build a long-term relationship of giving. The hardest part is getting a person to make the first gift. If he says yes, he's taking the hardest step. Thank him.

Creating a stewardship system

It is helpful to create a consistent stewardship system or checklist. Since thanking people feels like something that's important, but not urgent, it's easy to let it slide. Communicating gratitude may never get done. Having a checklist or automated reminders can help you do the right thing.

I've helped staff determine *who* contacts the donor and *what* kind of contact they make (note, phone call, visit …) for different gift sizes. A system like this is tedious to create but fairly simple to run.

Time spent here is as important as time spent in front of the donor making an ask.

In general, every single donor should get a formal gift receipt that he can use for his taxes. You might need to create this yourself or a national ministry office might do this for you. It's great if you are able to write a personal note on those or sign them. (I prefer using blue pens. I've heard people respond better to blue. This may be because it looks more "real" than something run through a printer.)

I'd encourage you to send him a separate thank-you note as well. It doesn't need to be long—just something thanking him for investing in the Kingdom through your ministry. I like to use a smaller card for this. The card stands out from all the other mail because it's not a business-sized envelope. Also, it looks full even with only two or three lines of writing. If you have a lot of donors, it might make sense to start the handwritten thank you notes at a specific gift level. There's no magic level; it needs to be based on what you can handle and how personally you want your donors to know your appreciation. Some set the level at $50, others at $100, others at $500. It's up to you.

At a higher level, donors should get a quick "thank-you" phone call. You are not harassing your donors; you're calling solely to say "thank you."

Many programs find it helpful to have some sort of celebration event to thank people. Events let people see other people who support the same ministry. But be careful. It's too easy to make these events about the ministry's staff when it needs to be about gratitude to the donors.

Also, (as you'll see in the chapter on personality styles) extroverts tend to love being up front or seeing their name on a donor list, while introverts often would feel more appreciated by enjoying a quiet tea with the head of the ministry. If you have an event in place, terrific! But if not, don't rush out to create one without thinking through the strategy first.

Not asking *for* prayer, but offering to *pray*

I once received an unexpected call from a ministry I financially supported. The caller said she was calling to thank me for partnering with the ministry. I guardedly said, "You're welcome." When she started speaking again, I thought, "Here we go. Here comes the ask for another donation."

But it didn't come.

She explained that the staff meets for prayer every morning. In addition to praying for the needs of the ministry, they pray over each of their partners. Again, I thought, "She mentioned 'needs' so I *know* there is an ask coming."

I was wrong again.

She did ask. But her ask blew me away. She said, "So I was wondering, would you like us to be praying for anything specific during that time?"

That blew my mind. I was surprised to find myself opening up to a complete stranger. I shared a few personal things they could put on the prayer card.

The best part was that she ended the call there. I kept waiting for the proverbial "other shoe" to drop, but it never did.

Adding telephone calls to your stewardship plan can be powerful even if you are unable to speak in person. I would have felt just as moved by a voice mail thanking me and asking if they could focus on any specific prayer needs.

The only thing that might have made it better would have been a follow-up call. "We've been praying for this situation for a month, how are things going?" This would have reminded me about the ministry at another time that I might have given. (I tend to make one-time donations rather than monthly ones.)

As a person fundraising for Christian ministry, you have the most amazing relationship tool in your toolkit: *prayer*. Unfortunately, too many people use prayer as a way of backing into asking for a gift. Don't ask people to "pray for your work" and follow with a "give to it, too." What if rather than asking *for* prayer, you *offered to pray*?

For too long, ministries have been seen as "takers" rather than "givers." Unfortunately, there is a lot of entitlement in the field. Too often fundraisers feel justified in rudely making their requests and expecting people to pay since they're "doing the Lord's work."

Prayer is a great way to overcome that. I stumbled upon this principle while working at a Christian boarding school. I'd grown tired of hearing, "I thought it was a *Christian* school. Why is it we only hear from the school when they're asking for money?" I wanted to shout, "Because if you all gave some, we wouldn't need to ask so much!!!" But I didn't think that would help build relationships, so I held my tongue.

Thinking about them adding "Christian" to the objection, I wondered what we could do to reinforce that aspect of our school in their minds. So I created an email "prayer list" alumni could join. On a regular basis, I'd email this intercessory group with general prayer requests based on the time of the year, asking people to pray for the students, the faculty, etc. There wasn't a hidden pitch for money. These were stand-alone emails solely requesting prayer. We kept the same fundraising schedule; we simply added these emails to the mix. I figured I could now honestly say that they didn't *only* hear from us about money!

One day, a student got so excited about alumni praying for the school, he asked, "Mr. Pitman, I know the alumni are praying for us. Can we pray for the alumni too?"

Awesome, isn't it?

So then I started regularly communicating with the alumni community (it was a Yahoo group at the time), "The students will be praying for you this week and want to know what needs each of you may have." Alumni could reply to the group or privately to me.

Only a few alumni participated. But it sent *all* the right messages. Not only was the school adding prayer to the mix:

- We weren't reliant on money but on God, and we knew that.

- We were able to get into the inboxes of alumni—even those who weren't Christians. We were reminding them about Jesus and the part the school played in their lives.

- We were connecting alumni with current students (not directly but as a group). And honestly, that's who alumni connected with anyway!

- We were able to directly "train" a group of future alumni while they were still on campus!

Now, I realize you may not be fundraising for a school or have a built-in constituency like alumni, but neither did the ministry that asked for my prayer requests.

Flavoring communications with gratitude

One of the rules of thumb in fundraising is that you should thank people at least *seven times* before you ask them again. This can be really challenging for fundraisers. I once had a well-meaning coaching client tell me she couldn't possibly send another direct mail solicitation because she hadn't thanked all her donors seven times yet! Following a rigid formula is not always helpful!

The point is not to stop all mailings until you are sure everyone has been thanked seven times. Nor does it mean you should send out seven "thank-you only" appeals between fundraising letters or say "thank you" seven times in rapid succession when we see a donor.

Thanking people at least seven times means you need to retool your donor communications so they come from a place of gratitude. Or perhaps I should say you "get" to. It's a lot more fun to communicate with donors from a position of gratitude rather than bragging. And gratitude is not groveling. You're not saying you're scum and he's some sort of superior master. Not at all.

It means you no longer feel driven to brag about what a great ministry *you* have and all the great work *you* do. Instead, all of your newsletters, interviews in the paper or on radio, and face-to-face meetings can be colored with gratefulness that people's gifts make our work possible. You may make subtle changes like, "Thanks to generous people like you ... " or more bold ones like, "See what you've done?" You have the privilege to connect the donors with the actual impact. That connection is real because, without them, your ministry's impact wouldn't be possible.

Now some of you are freaking out. I can hear you saying, "What?! I have to add a whole new layer of events and contacts to my already full schedule?!" That's a great question. I'll definitely argue that if your ministry is dependent on donors, this time with donors *is* part of your ministry. Do you see that "engagement" events can also double as "love" events? You're educating both prospects and donors on the sound judgment of investing in your ministry. If your engagement events include gratitude, your prospects will see that other people like them are already giving to your ministry. That is exactly the "social proof" people are looking for— evidence that others (especially people like themselves) have already done what you're inviting them to do.

I find it helpful to think of the Get R.E.A.L. process as a circle:

Research leads to engaging prospects. Engagement leads to making the ask. Asking leads to thanking donors—which inevitably loops back around to engaging them before the next gift.

Dealing with a "no"

You can see the "love" step is relatively easy if he says he'll make a gift. But what if after all your prayer and hard work he says, "No"? What do you do?

First, **don't take it personally!** It's very tempting to feel he is rejecting you. He's not. He's not rejecting you. He's not questioning your call. Maybe your appeal simply didn't land with him in a way that made him want to give. Or perhaps other things that you don't know about are going on with the donor. Do all you can to resist taking the "no" personally.

Next, **don't cross off the prospect from your list!** It can feel good to defensively, aggressively cross the prospect's name off your list and drop him from any future communication. You may think "If he's not going to play, forget him!"

No! No matter how badly you feel, you can't just write off people. *Your job in the ministry of fundraising is to develop lifelong relationships between your ministry and people from outside of your ministry.* You need to develop mutually beneficial relationships. There may be times to drop people from your list. But walking away from someone because he's said "no" to a solicitation is *not* an effective way to build a lifelong relationship.

As Christians, we know that *people are always more important than their gifts.* Stop right now and repeat it to yourself until you believe it: "People are always more important than their gifts."

There many legitimate reasons for saying no to you right now.

You've done the very best you can to match the prospect to your mission. You've attempted to show him the intersection of his values with your ministry. Be an adult and allow him to say no.

Do you remember the Gift Range Calculator? When you print it out, you will see you need up to five prospects for each gift. So you just succeeded in finding one of the five. Now it's time to trust God is leading you and move on.

Gracefully handling a rejection now may lead to a much larger gift later on. **A "no" now is simply that ... a "no" for now.** If you've done the researching and engaging effectively, you had some concrete reasons to ask for the gift, *so keep nurturing the relationship.* Prove to the prospect that you're interested in him as a person. This can be as simple as sending a note every few months. There may come a point when you stop interacting with the person (his interests may change, etc.), but don't cut off contact because you feel rejected.

I knew of a donor who became so disappointed with an employee leaving that she asked for her $40,000 gift back. That was about 10% of our annual fund! I'm proud of the decision made by the leaders of the organization. Rather than threatening legal action, they sent the gift back. That kind of decision takes integrity.

They also did an incredibly brilliant thing—they convened a team of three individuals to create a strategy to bridge the donor's interest from the former employee to the entire organization. Their strategy worked. Eighteen months after requesting her gift back, she made a pledge of half a million dollars. Even more importantly, a path was paved for a lifelong relationship. She spoke very movingly at a donor event about the importance of how God used the organization in her life.

What would have happened if the leaders had taken her to court in order to keep the $40,000? What if the leaders had told her there was no way they would give her gift back? They may have been able to keep the $40,000, but how much would it have cost them? How much would it have cost them if they wrote off the donor as a lost cause?

Like so much of fundraising, the "love" step is a good case of common sense. This rests on knowledge that's been around for millennia. Thousands of years ago, the revered rabbi Hillel said, "That which is hateful to you, do not do to others." A few centuries later, another rabbi named Jesus said, "Love others as you love yourself."

Fundraising is a relationship business. It's not about selling a t-shirt one time and moving on to find another customer. It's more like gardening. You need to plant seeds and nurture them as they grow. Just like in gardening, not all seeds grow at the same pace. Some need more time; some need less. Some are annuals needing more effort; some are perennials needing (or wanting) less in-your-face relationship building.

I once went to visit a donor who had been very generous to the school where I was employed. A few decades before, he had given a cumulative amount of $100,000. Since then he and the school had lost touch. I was shocked. Anyone who'd ever given $1000 in their life to the school was in the top 20% of all time donors! So how in the world had we let him go without even a personal note or visit? I was resolved to fix that.

When I got to the retirement community, I asked the receptionist to call him. She hesitated, but I didn't notice that until later. I thought it was odd that instead of calling the donor, the receptionist asked his wife to come down to meet me. As I waited, I looked back toward the entrance of the lobby. There facing me was a picture of the gentleman I was going to visit with the words "In Memory Of" along with the date of his birth and that day's date. It turned out he had passed away at 2 a.m.!

I didn't make any ask that day. This was one of those sacred moments I was blessed with as a fundraiser. I had no other appointments that morning, so I visited with his widow for three hours. I heard about their life together and the trips they had recently taken. I saw the pottery kiln he'd bought her and listened to stories about her kids. I was able to be with her in a way few others could. Everyone else who called or stopped by felt compelled to say something or to help, but they weren't sure quite what to say. Most resorted to asking about funeral details. I was able to simply be with her, pray for her, and listen to her. My appointment was definitely a divine appointment; God just had a different agenda for it than I did.

It is unlikely that you'll experience something quite this extreme, but I hope you let your donors know that you care about them just as much as you care about your ministry. Don't become so focused on the gift that you forget the giver.

One easy way to love on your donors is to ask them how and when they'd like to be asked. Honor that as much as possible. You can also find out how they'd like to be thanked. Many nonprofits have an annual dinner to showcase and honor their best donors, but some have asked their donors whether they *like* to be honored publicly. Many generous people enjoy giving quietly and staying away from the spotlight. The most meaningful way to thank them could involve taking them out to dinner or hosting a smaller reception at the executive director's house.

A Warning

Learn to create systems that make loving on your donors and

prospects habitual. Your objective is to raise money. You're not around to be the entertainment director or everybody's best friend. Successful fundraising is a constant tension between being politely relational and having a particular desired outcome for the relationship. You need to focus your efforts on a carefully selected group of people, *and* you need to do that while treating all the others with respect.

I'm convinced that those who learn to honor people more than their money will find their funding challenges getting smaller.

Now that you've learned the four "Get R.E.A.L." steps, let's take a look at some of the ways *not* to ask for money.

Chapter 5
Seven Fundraising Faux Pas

"A life spent making mistakes is
not only more honorable, but
more useful than a life spent
doing nothing."
> - George Bernard Shaw

"If I had to live my life again, I'd
make the same mistakes, only
sooner."
> - Tallulah Bankhead

"An expert is a person who has
made all the mistakes that can
be made in a very narrow field."
> - Niels Bohr

"Mistakes are the portals of
discovery."
> - James Joyce

"While one person hesitates
because he feels inferior, the
other is busy making mistakes
and becoming superior."
                    - Henry C. Link

"Mistakes are part of the dues
one pays for a full life."
                    - Sophia Loren

"To avoid situations in which
you might make mistakes may
be the biggest mistake of all."
                    - Peter McWilliams

I'm convinced that one of the best ways to learn what to do is by learning what *not* to do. Now that you've seen how to ask for money well, let's take a light-hearted look at seven of the most common mistakes I see fundraisers make. I should know—I've committed most of them!

Not only are these stories instructive, but they're also a lot of fun. I hope the humor will make them easier to remember *and* harder to repeat.

Fundraising Faux Pas #1:
The Field of Dreams Fiasco

During a client's board meeting, we stumbled upon the perfect opportunity to ask one of their donors to participate in planned giving. The person had been actively involved with the organization for years. Her planned gift could endow an annual scholarship that was already being given in honor of her parents.

This opportunity was so good that I was bursting with excitement! I enthusiastically explained how amazingly right a planned giving solicitation would be for this person. Such a gift might allow this donor to do for the organization what she hadn't been able to do up until now. The organization would benefit for decades to come from her generosity, and her extended family might even get involved and make gifts that would grow the fund over the years.

When I stopped to let them discuss who would set up the visit, an uncomfortable silence filled the room. They fidgeted and shuffled their papers. After what seemed like an eternity, one person hesitatingly said, "I'm not sure we should ask her *individually* ... What if we just sent a letter to our entire database asking them to consider a planned gift?"

One by one, everyone in the room began to breathe again. They all looked relieved, saying things like "Yeah, let's do that!" and "Great idea!" I was completely stunned. I was so surprised—I actually called them a bunch of chickens. (I had a very good relationship with this board!)

They'd fallen for the *Field of Dreams* fiasco. In the movie *Field of Dreams*, the refrain is "If you build it, they will come." A nonprofit variation is: "If you send it, they will give." It seems that nonprofit boards often think people will make a large gift simply because they receive a mass-produced letter.

Sending a solicitation letter *is* better than *not* sending one, but most people won't open the envelope. The vast majority of those who do open it will look to see if their name is on it (instead of the awful "Dear Valued Person") and then check the postscript. Very few will actually ever read the entire letter.

Here's the shocking truth about why: *your organization is not the center of your donors' universe.* They don't think about it nearly as much as you do. If the case for giving to the nonprofit were so self-evident, people would already be giving more than your organization could handle.

One of the concepts I stress to my clients is P.Y.I.T.S.—Put Yourself In Their Shoes. It's so important that I've dedicated the entire next chapter to this concept! Think about the situation above. If you received the planned giving letter they wanted to mail, would you be motivated to talk to an attorney about changing your will? Of course not.

It would probably take many letters over time from an organization you love to make you go through this discomfort. That's why in the direct mail world a 1% response rate is quite good. That means if you get one gift for every 100 letters, the mailing was successful by direct mail standards.

Here's a tip: If you're doing a campaign or asking a donor for a big gift, resist the urge just to send a one-size-fits-all mass mailing. Don't say, "if everyone gave just $100 we'd raise the total amount." Decades of fundraising experience across the nonprofit sector shows this doesn't work. Use the steps in this book, particularly the chapters on research and engagement, to successfully reach your goal. Isn't your organization worth it?

Fundraising Faux Pas #2:
The Mickey D's Syndrome

When a dear family friend moved into senior housing, we had to get everything out of her house. Her new apartment was full long before the house was empty. With all the additional stuff on the lawn, it felt like we were starring on an episode of the TV show *Clean Sweep*.

To save time, I rented a dumpster. Rather than the cute little green one I'd thought I'd ordered, a huge construction-sized monster dumpster showed up in her yard. And it was a good thing, too! This woman was a bargain hunter *and* a pack rat. We threw out enough "seen on TV" gizmos and gadgets to fill up about half of the dumpster.

Only once did she get really upset—when I threw out a kitty litter bucket that actually contained an expensive compost starter. The thought struck me that if she hadn't spent so much money on "good deals"(which she never used) she would have been able to buy bucket loads of compost starter.

This hoarding mentality and buying things just because they

seem cheap are forms of "poverty thinking." Nonprofits get stuck in this poverty thinking all the time. They become so focused on stretching their money that they lose sight of quality. They will put the cheapest cabinets in a multimillion-dollar building. Or they will bring their major donor to McDonald's to show her how frugal they are. (Seriously. This has happened.)

Most donors, especially major donors, know that paying a little more up front will save significant amounts of money down the road. Cheap cabinets may have saved a few bucks this year, but they'll be destroyed with a year of heavy use and need to be replaced. Buying a more expensive cabinet and higher quality cabinets will actually save money over time because they won't need to be replaced as soon.

The same idea applies when it comes to cultivating donors. Paying a little more up front can save lots of money over time. Taking a donor out to a nice restaurant is a way of showing her that you value her. Her relationship means more to you than just the money she is giving. She needs to know that you care about her and share her interests.

Here's a tip: If a donor means enough to your organization to take her out to dinner, go to a place with real silverware and cloth napkins! Show her how well you stewarded the money she gave, but don't be a cheapskate.

Fundraising Faux Pas #3:
The Cheez-It Treatment

Have you tried to buy a box of Cheez-Its in the supermarket? A short time ago, I did. I found the process incredibly intimidating; there are more than ten different kinds of Cheez-Its! Some of the varieties to choose from included:

- Original

- Reduced Fat

- White Cheddar

- Big Cheez-Its

- Cheesy Sour Cream and Onion

- Parmesan and Garlic

- Cheddar Jack

- SpongeBob Cheez-Its

- Party Mix

- Chili Cheese

- Hot and Spicy

It took so long to look at the wall of orangish-red boxes that I almost forgot what kind I wanted to buy. The choice overwhelmed me enough that I felt paralyzed at first. Then I felt stupid. How was it that I, a guy with a Master's degree, couldn't make a simple choice about a box of crackers?

Not liking to feel stupid, I left the aisle.

You might inadvertently give your donor the Cheez-Its Treatment by overwhelming him with giving options. If you're afraid that this might be the only time you get in front of her, you may think that the more options you present, the better. Instead, you are giving her so many options that you're probably confusing her.

For example, your web page or direct mail letter may give donors the options something like this:

> "You can give __$1000, __ $500, __$100, __$50, __$25, __$12.50, or __any amount."

Or it may also include a check box next to text like this:

> *"Please send me information on planned giving, stock transfers, creating an endowment, and corporate matching gifts."*

Both examples are bad. The intentions are good. Options can be helpful, but neuroscience reveals a caveat. Although people like making choices, they stop deciding when presented with too many options. People would rather not act than act and look stupid.

So remember: P.Y.I.T.S.—put yourself in their shoes. Think about it from the donor's perspective: Are all these options motivating her to give or are they paralyzing her?

Here's a tip: Try limiting the options for giving to three or four. Instead of sending a letter to all your donors listing giving options from $10-$10,000, you can categorize donor lists and send slightly different reply cards with only three options. Use an amount close to what they gave last year, a larger amount, and an even larger amount than that. The donor may surprise you and give an amount much greater than you expected.

Fundraising Faux Pas #4:
Mrs. McTat's House of Cats

We have to watch what we say. In the children's book *Mrs. McTat and Her Houseful of Cats*, kids are taught the alphabet while being mesmerized by a great story about a kind lady who eventually collects 26 cats. Sharing a home with 26 cats may send shivers down your spine, but it's possible that your donor loves cats. So you have to choose your words carefully.

Stephen Nill, founder and CEO of CharityChannel.com, wonderfully illustrates this point in one of his tales (that sounds a lot like Mrs. McTat) from the campaign trail:

> *I was meeting with an elderly lady, 89 years*
> *old, who had around 20 cats in her home and*
> *around her property. She was contemplating a*
> *very large gift to an organization for which I*
> *was consulting as a planned giving officer.*
>
> *The conversation was going very well. Then,*
> *she asked how to go about making a planned*
> *gift. For reasons that are now lost in the fog*
> *of time, I said, "There's more than one way to*
> *skin a cat."*
>
> *You don't want to know what happened next.*
> *It was ugly. Really, really ugly.*

I couldn't stop laughing when I read this. How many times have we wished we could take back something we have said? You can't assume (yes, never assume) anything. Not everyone loves cats like Mrs. McTats, and not everyone loathes the animal either.

I find this to be particularly true with politics. People tend to hang out with others who believe and vote like they do. Don't forget your donors may not share all of your values and opinions. Be careful not to unnecessarily alienate your donor by glibly saying things that your friends and colleagues would whole-heartedly support.

Here's a tip: Script your key questions and answers *before* your visit. Practice repeating them to your steering wheel as you drive around.

As I mentioned earlier in the book, phrases that may seem ordinary to you may not fit the situation. Be flexible and open to using different phrases. In fact, creating this kind of script actually *increases* your flexibility and frees you up to enjoy the other person more.

But isn't it somewhat reassuring that none of us wins them all?

Fundraising Faux Pas #5:
The Spell-Check-Will-Catch-It Faux Pas

It's easy to rely only on spell-check to catch your mistakes—until it doesn't catch one and you're wearing egg all over your face. *Spell-check is not the same as proofreading.* Here are a couple of short stories from development professionals regarding follies with spell-check:

> I used the word "erotic" when I meant "erratic." Luckily it wasn't in a situation where it could do any damage!
>
> ---
>
> Probably the worst I can remember was in a mailing to major donors, when I learned the word public does not show up on spell check if you leave out the "l"!

We've all been there, haven't we? You work on a letter. Read it over. And over. And over. You edit it again and again. Finally, you print it and mail it. Then, when you get our own copy in the mail, you see mistakes like those mentioned above!

Here's a tip: Most people aren't great at proofreading their own work. Your brain feels sorry for you. It helps you "see" what you think is there rather than what is actually written. You need to get someone who hasn't even seen the letter to read it. Better still— get someone outside of your organization who doesn't speak your jargon. See if she can understand the letter. If you've ever done this, isn't it embarrassing how many mistakes you've missed?

While computers are wonderful tools, they can't read your mind. Two sets of eyes are always better than one. You'll especially appreciate this when someone else catches something that you didn't see after staring at the page for hours.

Fundraising Faux Pas #6:
The You're-Good-Enough-To-Go-It-Alone Blunder

On a recent fundraising campaign, I fell prey to one of the classic blunders: *letting a solicitor fly solo.* (For you *Princess Bride* fans, this classic blunder comes immediately after "Never go in against a Sicilian when death is on the line.")

This particular solicitor was wonderfully gifted and incredibly connected in the community. She had been an active volunteer and fundraiser for our organization for decades. As the development person, I was paired up with her for the campaign solicitations.

When I called her to see how the contacts were going and let her know I was available to go with her anytime she would like, she declined my help. She knew all the people personally but thanked me for my offer. We hung up, both feeling good about ourselves, about the campaign, and about life in general.

Then I realized the problem: *we were asking people for considerably more money than anyone had ever given our organization.* These asks were going to be uncomfortable, and I was letting her fly into this unknown territory without me there by her side to support her. Worse yet, without an accountability person, it was far easier for her to chicken out and settle for a much lower ask amount.

I wasn't sure how to rectify this situation until she dropped by my office a few days later. I immediately said, "I'm *so* sorry." "For what?" she asked, somewhat surprised. "For leaving you all by yourself to make these calls! I do this asking for a living, but you don't." I told her I was committed to helping her make the solicitations and would clear my schedule to be with her during her calls.

She was visibly relieved. She still needed to make the calls for appointments because she had stronger relationships with our prospective donors. But I was back in as an aide and accountability person. I was also with her at the solicitations; I made sure that the ask was specific for the predetermined dollar amount.

Here's a tip: Pair up as much as possible for all of the asks. Making solicitations as a pair is much more effective than going it alone. It puts everyone in the room at ease, including you.

Fundraising Faux Pas #7:
The Highway Fallacy

The highway fallacy comes from that ultimatum: "My way or the highway!"

In fundraising, this is when you're so committed to going in and getting a gift that you entirely ignore all the clues the donor gives about their own values and interests. Ignoring these clues is a sure way to fail quickly when you're making an ask.

If you go to a solicitation, and the donor is clearly not interested, stop. Put down your presentation materials and let her know that you can see she's distracted. Offer to come back at a more opportune time.

Who knows? Perhaps her child is in labor with her first

grandchild. Or maybe a family member took a turn for the worse the night before. Whatever the case, your organization is worthy of her complete attention. She'll probably be grateful for your consideration.

I'll get into this in much more detail in the next two chapters "P.Y.I.T.S." and "Know Your Donors." For now, remember that *not everyone is like you*. Your organization isn't the most important thing in your donor's world.

Here's a tip: Run your ideas past a coach, colleague, or trusted friend (particularly someone who sees things from a different perspective than you). Get her honest opinion, and be willing to listen to the feedback.

In Conclusion
Individually, none of these faux pas will ruin your fundraising. But commit all of them and you may be lucky if you raise any money at all!

You can avoid making major mistakes by remembering the following:

- Don't be lulled into thinking everyone understands your cause.
- Don't be cheap with your major donors.
- Don't overwhelm people with too many options.
- Don't forget to be careful with your phrasing.
- Don't fail to have someone else look over your letters.
- Don't go alone on major asks.
- Don't ignore the clues the donor is sending you.

Chapter 6
Put Yourself in Their Shoes

"Some people think only
intellect counts: knowing how
to solve problems, knowing
how to get by, knowing how to
identify an advantage and seize
it. But the functions of intellect
are insufficient without
courage, love, friendship,
compassion and empathy."
                    - Dean Koontz

"The great gift of human beings
is that we have the power of
empathy."
                    - Meryl Streep

"Do to others as you would have
them do to you. "
                    - Jesus, Luke 6:13

"Friendship is a living thing
that lasts only as long as it
is nourished with kindness,
empathy and understanding."
                    - Unknown

"The most valuable things in life
are not measured in monetary
terms. The really important
things are not houses and
lands, stocks and bonds,
automobiles and real state, but
friendships, trust, confidence,
empathy, mercy, love and faith."
          - Bertrand Russell V. Delong

Throughout the chapters on the Get R.E.A.L. process, I repeatedly referred to "P.Y.I.T.S." In this chapter, let's take a closer look at how *putting yourself in their shoes* can make your fundraising far more effective.

I once had a colleague who wrote an end-of-the-year letter that drove home the importance of P.Y.I.T.S. He was a "numbers person" who wrote the letter with the statistics and facts that would motivate him. He'd worked for weeks on crafting this letter. The main thrust of the letter was something like this:

> *Alumni, we need to raise more money. The parents*
> *have nearly reached their goal at 90 percent, but the*
> *alumni have only raised 20 percent of their goal.*
> *We really need your help to pull this thing together.*

After a couple of us read it, we gathered up our courage, went to his office, closed the door, and told him we thought it was … *terrible.*

As we were reading the letter, we'd put ourselves in the shoes of the people who would be receiving the letter. We thought about how we would feel if we didn't work with this nonprofit and we'd received this in the mail. We found ourselves thinking things like: "That's not my problem." and "I don't care what your goals are—sounds like you're not too good at setting them."

A letter like this was not going to encourage us (or anyone else, for that matter) to give. Knowing how skilled this fundraiser normally was, I was quite surprised by my strong negative reaction.

In an effort to help our colleague, we asked him why he was so committed to the school. We knew he had *wired* his first annual gift from Europe the year after he graduated from the prep school. How many college freshmen wire gifts to their former school? He was now working at his alma mater, and his kids were getting ready to enroll. We asked him what motivated him and encouraged him to tell his story.

It was a pretty uncomfortable conversation. But he ended up writing an amazingly moving letter—even though it was totally out of his comfort zone. We raised more money than we had ever raised at the end of the year. You know you've written an effective appeal when people put notes in with their checks telling you that they were crying as they read the letter. People wrote to tell us that his story reminded them how this school had impacted their lives and their kids' lives. This moved them to make a gift. That success all came from putting ourselves in their shoes *before* we sent the letter.

Budget Crisis or Manipulating Donors?

Many years ago I made a one-time gift to a large national nonprofit. Every December after that, I received a strongly worded, emotional appeal for money. The letters basically said, "We're not going to make our budget if you don't help us out now."

The first time I saw this letter, I felt bad for the organization. I didn't make a gift, but it saddened me to think that the great work I'd invested in wouldn't be able to continue. After three years of receiving these letters, I called them up and said, "If you guys are that fiscally unsound, and you can't manage the money you've been given, I can't even consider giving you another gift. Please remove me from your mailing list."

They were shocked at my reaction. They'd been mailing this package for years. It was their "control package"—the letter that always brought in the most gifts. It was actually sent halfway through their fiscal year so they still had plenty of fundraising time in front of them. However, they sent the appeal in December since most of their donations came in during that month.

If you have a sincere budget crisis, then, by all means, tell your donors! Bad things happen to the best causes. But don't keep warning about the dire possibility of not making your budget. That's not the donors' problem; that's your problem. Crying "Wolf!" is a sure-fire way to get people to ignore you. Development isn't about meeting your needs; it's really about *meeting your donors' needs.* You're expected to be fiscally competent enough to balance a budget. Your job is to show them the impact their gift is making.

So, before you send out a letter or make a solicitation, take a moment to *put yourself in their shoes* by asking yourself, "How would I feel if I didn't work with this ministry and I were approached in this way?"

Taking the time to ask this one question will make your fundraising more effective, and it will save you a lot of heartache.

Take Time
Much of direct mail fundraising is focused on getting people to *actually* open the envelope. Some direct mail research seems to indicate that if you don't have a return address on the envelope, people will open it because they don't want to miss out on something. One organization that practices this method crafted an entire campaign around the theme "CREDIT DENIED." The idea behind it was to share the story of a family that needed financial help and couldn't get it—their credit was denied. But thanks to donor support this organization was able to help them. The story moved everyone in the organization. "CREDIT DENIED" became their battle cry.

To keep the entire direct mail package tied to this theme, they printed the outside of the envelopes with big red letters "Credit Denied!" Unfortunately, no one thought about what it would be like to get such a letter in his or her mailbox. When people went to their mailboxes and found a letter with "CREDIT DENIED" stamped on it with no return address, they definitely opened it. But when they found out it was a fundraising appeal, they got ticked off before they even were able to read the terrific story! When a colleague shared this story with me on a CharityChannel. com listserv, there were comments from people on the list who cut the organization out of their annual giving because of that very mailing! They still remembered their shock and anger years later!

It seemed like a good idea. It even made sense from an organizational perspective, but the tagline on the envelope scared people about their own credit so much that they weren't even interested in reading an appeal. The outcome could have been dramatically different if someone in the organization had assembled a sample mailing and then asked, "How might I feel if I received this in my mailbox?"

I like to remind clients that their organization is *not* the center of their donors' universe. Much of the lives of board members and employees revolves around their cause, but donors have lives of their own. Things that are self-evident to solicitors are not necessarily self-evident to donors.

It's easy to get so consumed with reaching your goals and coming up with catchy ideas that you don't take the time to think about what others will see when they receive your material. Just taking a few minutes to think about the people you're trying to reach—to put yourself in their shoes—can save you from myopically doing more damage than good with your appeals.

Conversational or Scripted?

Do you remember the #1 reason people don't give? *They're not asked.*

While I'm not exactly the biggest proponent of phonathons, I believe they can be an effective way of asking. I've had to run them from time-to-time. If you've ever participated in a phonathon, you usually have a script when you make the calls. But those scripts can make college graduates sound like a bad Saturday Night Live skit: "Hi … my … name is … Marc … I'm calling on be … half of … " That's not exactly the way to impress prospective donors—particularly if you're fundraising for a school!

The callers sound unprofessional and impersonal. Put yourself in the donor's shoes. If you're on the other end of the phone, you know when someone is reading a script to you. Wouldn't you rather give to someone who is having a conversation with you?

Why not help phonathon participants sound like friends? If you're running a phonathon, have a complete, word-for-word script. Calling can be nerve-wracking, and knowing exactly what is expected for each call is helpful. Add a section of bulleted key points so callers can quickly return to them. These fundamentals can be written on the top of the script, on separate index cards, or even on posters on the walls. If they could only do three things in the call, what would you want them to do? Then put it in the bullets. (Hint: asking for a gift should be one of those three!)

I recorded a quick video that can help you with calling donors. You can see it at: http://youtu.be/YpcZcwP3lKY

Comfortable in Your Own Shoes

Putting yourself in others' shoes is good. It's also good to get comfortable in your own shoes. You have to come to grips with the reality that you need to ask people to give money to your cause. At some point, you have to face your own fear and insecurities.

Whether you've been involved in fundraising for 30 days or 30 years, think about the times you were afraid. Just before you make the call to set up the appointment, what is your mind picturing? Often it's picturing the worst possible outcome. "I'm probably interrupting their busy schedule." Or "I bet they hate hearing from me."

Fear is your imagination going on the dark side and thinking about all the things that could go wrong. Usually, the things you were afraid of never happened anyway. Do you remember Mark Twain's quote:

> "I am an old man and have known a great many troubles, but most of them never happened."

That's the way it is with fear. Many of the negative things you picture won't ever happen.

So the next time you go to pick up the phone, ask God to fill you, and remind yourself that "perfect love drives out fear" (1 John 4:18). Imagine yourself making someone's day by asking him to give; you're helping him invest his resources in a cause he really cares about and values. This is just as "real" for your imagination as the fear pictures. And it's truer for donors. The positives far outweigh the negatives when it comes to giving people an opportunity to do something worthwhile with their money.

To help you get comfortable with what you are doing, begin by asking yourself, "Why am I asking for money?" This will drive you back to the "Research" step of the Get R.E.A.L. process.

Are you doing it to change a kid's life? Are you changing your community? There could be a thousand reasons for why you believe in your cause and asking for money to support it. Focusing on the positive outcomes will help you get over your fear. You may still be a little nervous, but at least you will be encouraged by the reminder of *why* you're making the ask.

And really, what is the worst that could happen? They could say "no." That's it. They're not going to lash out at you or collapse from shock. If they do say "no," they aren't rejecting you! They are just saying no to your request. And remember, their "no" is often simply a "no for now."

What if your ask is met with the donor's immediate "Yes."? Obviously, you thank them. But consider this: When I was starting out in fundraising, I heard the story of a fundraiser who asked for $1,000. The donor immediately wrote out the check without even thinking about it. This fundraiser was so comfortable in his own shoes and committed to his ministry, that he handed the check back! He told the donor, "I'm sorry. We didn't ask for enough. We don't want to be one of your throwaway charities. We want to be on your top 10 list." The businessman was taken aback. But this earned his respect. He knew they weren't just glad-handing, and that they were serious about what they did with his money.

Giving the check back may not be the wisest thing. But if you're comfortable enough with yourself, you may decide to apply the technique discussed in Chapter 4. When someone easily commits to the amount you asked for too quickly, you ask as calmly and as smoothly as possible, " … a year for the next 3 years?" Suddenly, a $500 gift can turn into a $1,500 gift, and you don't have to go back to that person asking for money each year.

This really works! During one campaign, I'd called a donor to set up the solicitation. We'd had a nice tour of the facility, and she knew the call was coming. As we agreed on the time, she told me she'd already written the check. My heart sank. For some reason, I assumed it was for $250! I quickly regained my composure, put the smile back on my face (people can "hear" the smile over the phone!), and asked, "May I ask you a question that might be a bit impertinent?" She chuckled and said I could. "Would you consider writing that same check next November?" She chuckled again and said she would consider it.

When we met, she handed me a check for $2500—not the $250 that I'd imagined! This was the first gift she'd ever made to our organization, and that was a huge gift for our first-time givers. Then she told me she would write a check for the same amount next year. "You know, I would never have thought of it," she told me, "but I will do it because you asked." She was pleased to find that a $5000 gift in our campaign merited listing on a plaque. And I was ecstatic. Having this family's name on our campaign was definitely going to help us reach other people in our community!

So as you go through the Get R.E.A.L. process of asking for money, learn to get comfortable in your own shoes. And remember to **P.Y.I.T.S.—put yourself in their shoes,** too. If *you* wouldn't like receiving what you're about to give, chances are the other person won't either. So change your approach!

Chapter 7
Tools for Knowing Your Supporters

"Dreams are the touchstones of
our character."
- Henry David Thoreau

"We should take care not to
make the intellect our god;
it has of course, powerful
muscles, but no personality."
- Albert Einstein

"Always keep an open mind and
a compassionate heart."
- Phil Jackson

One of the biggest obstacles to overcome in fundraising is getting to know who your donors are. Sounds odd, doesn't it? You're probably already saying, "Hold on, Marc. I know *exactly* who my donors are, thank you very much. They're the ones who have made a gift to my ministry! I can print out a list of their names any time I want." I agree that it is important to keep good records! But what can you tell me *about* your donors? What are they like? Old? Young? Wealthy? Middle-class? Male? Female? Professionals? Blue collar? Single? Married? Parents? Business executives? Entrepreneurs? Smart? Savvy? Skilled? Generous? Do they tend to be optimists? Or pessimists? Do they like public recognition? Or do they prefer one-on-one appreciation?

Knowing as much as you can about the people you are inviting to care about your cause can go a long way in helping you achieve your goals—especially your goals of building long-term, mutually beneficial relationships. In this chapter, I'll introduce you to two practical assessments that can help you interact in every step of the Get R.E.A.L. process: the D.I.S.C. test and The Highlands Ability Battery. I'll also give you tools that you can use right now to know your donors better.

The D.I.S.C. Test

If you've never heard of the "D.I.S.C." test, you are missing out on an incredibly simple assessment tool that will help you understand people's personalities. These four personality classifications have been around for millennia. The labels change (ranging from the standard "sanguine," "phlegmatic," "melancholy," and "choleric" labels of the ancient Greeks to different kinds of cars or animals), but the basic quadrants are the same. I think it is enduring because this format is easy to grasp in a few paragraphs, yet something you can use for years.

To start learning about the D.I.S.C. assessment, take out a piece of paper and draw a circle with two lines through it (see the diagram below). The *vertical line* represents how fast or slow you process things. Write "faster" at the top of the circle and "slower" at the bottom. The *horizontal line* represents your preference of working with people or tasks. Write "tasks" on the left-hand side of the circle. Write "people" on the right. Each of these lines acts as a spectrum. Some people will be task oriented but not to the same extreme as others.

In your circle with the two lines, put a "D" in the upper left-hand quadrant; an "I" in the upper right-hand; an "S" in the lower right; and a "C" in the lower left. Your diagram should look like this one from the people at Personality Insights.

Image courtesy of PersonalityInsights.com

I recommend you take an official assessment by a provider (I've included some providers in the resource section). If you haven't taken the assessment, take a minute to evaluate where you might place yourself on the chart.

- Do you tend to be a faster-paced person? Do you prefer to be up front and on stage?
- Or do you prefer remaining behind the scenes and out of the limelight?
- Do you prefer interacting with people?
- Or do you take greater interest in the important tasks you're accomplishing?

Do you have an idea where you might be? Remember, the lines are spectrums; some people are more like the description, some less. People often tend to be a blend of two quadrants. Now let's look at each quadrant individually.

A Quick D.I.S.C. Overview

D's are people who are upfront and on stage. They're no-nonsense doers. They get things done, no matter what ... even if some may be offended. These folks are often what people think of as the stereotypical "leader." They're the people who say, "We're doing this *my* way." If you remember the the comic strip *Peanuts*, Lucy is a quintessential D.

I's are also upfront individuals, but they are very people-focused. I's just love being around other people. Like golden retrievers, I's strangers are just friends they haven't met yet. If they have to choose between coffee with friends or working on a task alone, they'll choose coffee with a friend. They're high-energy people who say, "We're going to have fun!" In *Peanuts*, Snoopy is a good example of an I.

S's also err on the side of people, but they don't want to be up front. S's are solid, dependable people. They want to make sure everyone's in harmony. They tend to have a great perspective on how people are feeling. We need S's because D's and I's tend to be so far out in front that they can be out of touch with how people are feeling and can run roughshod over them. And (as we'll see) C's aren't particularly wired to consider people's feelings. So S's are vital to every team. S's like to ask, "How is everyone doing?" Charlie Brown is a good example of an S.

C's are into getting tasks done correctly. They don't necessarily have a need or desire to be around people—especially when they're working. They study and research before coming to conclusions. They want to make sure everything is done correctly. They'll ask tons of questions to make sure a plan will work. They're great engineers and CPAs. They're the kind of people who say, "We're going to do it the *right* way, and *my* way is the right way." In *Peanuts*, a possible C is Schroeder. He's methodical, dedicated, precise, and usually practicing.

If you're a movie buff, then here is how a few characters' personalities might fit on the D.I.S.C. wheel:

- In "Gone with the Wind," Rhett Butler is a D, Ashley is an S.

- In the movie "Patch Adams," Robin Williams' character would be a high I.

- Professor Higgins from "My Fair Lady" is a stereotypical C.

This is just a broad-brush sketch. People write entire books on this. But this is enough for our purposes. Let's take a look at how people communicate and process information within each category.

D.I.S.C. at Work

Shortly after I began a new job, my wife and I learned that we were pregnant. Naturally, one of my wife's first assignments for me was to find out if my employer had any "paternity leave" policy. I felt extremely uncomfortable about asking since I had just started there. I thought about directly asking our CFO (he oversaw the human resources function), but I decided against it. He took things very seriously and (it seemed to me) a bit negatively. I didn't want to stir anything up, so I decided to send a personal "just-checking-but-I-know-this-probably-isn't-an-option" email to someone else in his office.

The *very next day*, I received a *policy statement* from the CFO himself! Not a note from the employee. Not a note from the CFO. A *policy statement!* I was angry and embarrassed! I hadn't even asked *him*. I had intentionally chosen not to ask him because I was sure I'd get a response like the one in front of me.

There was *nothing* personal in the email. There was nothing in there indicating that he knew I wasn't looking to get out of working my new job. There was no acknowledgment that my query had been merely informational. There was nothing about me at all! There was just a full-blown, bureaucratic, policy statement. I was beside myself!

Can you tell that I'm a high I? I took this impersonal response to mean that the CFO questioned my integrity and thought I was a slacker. After I'd vented to my boss and taken some time to cool off, I took my grievance to the CFO.

He had *no idea* that he had done anything that would upset me. "I was just writing policy," he said. "Every organization needs policies to run." Of course, he was right. Every organization does need policies. But it needs people, too!

If I had stepped back to see the situation in terms of D.I.S.C., I would have realized he was a high C. As such, he was more focused on policies and procedures (the task side of life) than relating to people. In an organization, C's know that you need some level of policies to help direct relationships within the organization. I would have also realized that this person was hired specifically because the organization was full of policy gaps. A high C was needed to fix them. My question revealed another gap, so he quickly filled it.

To a high I, like myself, his filling the gap felt more like he was playing a game of Whack-a-Mole, and I was the mole! Even after our call, he was mystified by my response—amazed that anyone would get emotionally upset by a policy.

We never did see eye-to-eye on that. However, we worked together, so we learned to get along. We had to. But a donor doesn't have to. So as a solicitor, you need to learn to get along with the donor more quickly and avoid interactions like this.

D.I.S.C. & Fundraising

Think about D.I.S.C. in terms of your donors. Can you see that knowing *how* to relate to someone will help you to be much more effective in asking him for money? If you're a high C, you'll probably tell your organization's story based on statistics, graphs, and columns of numbers. But if your prospect is a high I, she would rather hear about how your organization's work impacted one person's life. This is why the Engage step of the Get R.E.A.L. process is so important. You can pick up a lot of the cues here.

I'm a high I and a high D. I guess that means I'm a 100% fast motor person! Seminar attendees tell me I talk *very* fast. They usually ask me to slow down so they have a chance to catch up.

I *love* people, but (as a high D) completing tasks is also very important to me. One of the most frustrating fundraising visits for me was with a donor who was a high S. She spent *hours* touring me around her city. *Hours.*

I kept thinking about all the other donors I could have visited. At that point in my career, my goal was to pack my schedule with as many appointments as possible. I wanted to justify my travel with lots of visits and lots of solicitations. I thought appointments were more about task completion than about building relationships. I wanted to complete as many as I could to prove that I was wasn't wasting time.

As a Certified Franklin Covey Coach, I should have remembered Stephen Covey saying that with people, "Slow is fast; fast is slow." During my appointment with this donor, I needed to slow down. She was investing in our relationship. She was thrilled to have a representative from my organization come and visit her, and she wanted to treat me well. It turns out that taking that time with her created a relationship that produced fruit in the coming years. We're still in touch today.

As a fundraiser, you should take an assessment to get a real perspective of your personality. You'll be a much better fundraiser as you remind yourself that not everyone thinks like you. Using D.I.S.C., you can quickly identify where the donor prospect might be. If you're normally a slower speaker, you'll need to step it up with a fast-paced person just to keep your prospect from becoming bored. If you're usually faster paced, you'll want to slow down for people who linger over life rather than consume it. Your fast speech may come across as pushy. If you're a task person, you'll need to work really hard to include people stories for your I and S prospects. But if you're an I or S asking a C or D, you'll need to get to the point and be ready to back up your stories with facts. Facts that you (fortunately) have in the case statement you wrote in the "Research" step of the Get R.E.A.L. process!

With all these differences, can you see why I strongly suggest doing solicitations in pairs?

The Highlands Ability Battery

Another incredibly useful tool that will give you a way to approach your donors (as well as your own life) is The Highlands Ability Battery. This assessment revolutionized my own professional growth and my marriage.

In *First Break All the Rules,* authors Marcus Buckingham and Curt Coffman explain the difference between average managers, good managers, and great managers. The book takes on the common human resource myth that you need to work on your weaknesses and be a well-rounded person to succeed. Backed by all the statistical research of the Gallup Organization, Buckingham and Coffman show that great managers don't focus on people's weaknesses. Excellent managers discover people's natural strengths and put people in positions that let those strengths flourish.

The Highlands Ability Battery helps you do just that. It is specifically designed to help identify your "hard-wired" natural abilities. Natural abilities are the things that come easily to you. Most often, the stress you feel in life comes from either operating in areas that do not come naturally to you or from not using your abilities. As you arrange your lives more in line with your natural talents, you find stress practically evaporates, and your work becomes filled with a renewed energy and purpose.

Through a three-to-four-hour test full of nineteen seemingly mind-numbing work samples you have to complete within set time limits, the Highlands measures which tasks you complete quickly and which tasks take more of your time. Everyone could complete all the tasks if given enough time. The ones that you quickly complete indicate your hard-wiring—your natural talents.

One of the things I love most about the Highlands is that you can't skew the results. All the other personality assessments I've used ask you to rate yourself on what you perceive your behavior or attitudes to be. After you take a few, you begin to see where the questions are going and how to make the results look more as you would like. The Highlands is different. It objectively measures how well you perform on specific work samples. That's it. Either you do them in the allotted time, or you don't. There's no bias to it, so this method very effectively identifies your hard-wired, natural abilities.

After taking the test, you receive a very long report describing your results and how they affect your life. Then you have a two-hour, one-on-one feedback session with a coach. This coach has studied your results and is able to explain them. Together, you identify patterns or "clusters" of abilities which help you begin to strategize your life around your natural talents.

After completing the Highlands Ability Battery, my mother said, "Marc, I felt more mentally alert after spending 33 hours in labor with you than I do after taking this test! I hope it's worth it!" Fortunately, it was. After seeing the report and going over it with a knowledgeable coach, my mom was amazed. The Highlands helped her explain some learning styles she had noticed in herself but hadn't been able to put into words. It helped her see herself in a completely new light.

And how did it revolutionize my marriage? It gave my wife and me a common language based on an objective assessment. One of the abilities measured is *idea productivity*. Idea productivity measures how fast your faucet of ideas is flowing, not whether the ideas are good or bad. Some people are generating new ideas all the time; others generate very few. Neither is better than the other. Some roles require coming up with lots of ideas quickly. But people with high idea productivity can't always focus; all the new ideas keep distracting them.

I'm a mid-range in idea productivity; my wife is off the charts! The other day, she and I were talking at the kitchen table as she was eating some store-bought pudding. All of a sudden, she stopped talking in mid-sentence, staring at her empty plastic cup. Just staring at it. It was really weird. I thought I had lost her. I was hoping I hadn't done something to offend her!

Then she snapped out of it. "Sorry," she said. "Idea productivity. I just had about a hundred ideas of what I could do with this little plastic cup." Immediately the whole situation made sense, and I was able to relax. That's just how she lives her life—ideas coming in a constant flow. People who have high idea productivity have hundreds of ideas thrown against the front of their brain all the time. The ideas aren't all good, but the quantity can be overwhelming.

Think about this regarding donor relations. Do you have a donor or alumnus who is always coming up with ideas on how you can do your job better? Maybe she's simply high in idea productivity. Rather than letting her grate on your nerves, why not invite her to the next staff brainstorming session? Her hard-wired ability may help improve whatever you're discussing. And if you're asking her for money, you know you'll need to vary your approach with props, other people, and other tools just to help her stay focused.

Let's look at some of the abilities the Highlands evaluates and see how these can affect your approach to fundraising.

Highlands: Introvert and Extrovert

The only subjective part of the Highlands is the portion that evaluates whether you are an introvert or an extrovert. Knowing this can help avoid many conflicts! Introverts tend to share an idea once they've worked through it internally and arrived at their finished product. They've thought things over, come to a resolution, framed it, and now they're through. Extroverts, on the other hand, start talking without knowing what the finished idea will be. They love doing the processing outside themselves and with others. Extroverts practically have to speak to think.

Guess what happens when an introvert shares an idea with a group of people. Extroverts in the group pounce on the idea like a cat pouncing on a ball of yarn. They don't realize the introvert was sharing a completed thought, not a rough draft. From an introvert's perspective, who would be crazy enough to share an idea that hadn't been thought through completely? The idea she shared was meant to be a finished product. And now the insensitive extroverts are shredding it apart!

We've all been in this situation before. When teams learn this introvert/extrovert distinction brought out by the Highlands, extroverts start asking things like, "Is this a rough draft or a polished idea?" Introverts also get less offended when an extrovert runs with an idea because they understand that not everyone processes the same way they do.

Another difference between introverts and extroverts is what tends to stimulate them. Extroverts tend to get energy from people; introverts tend to get energy from being alone. Since extroverts are energized by people, they prefer to be spontaneous in their interactions with others. An extrovert can be like a golden retriever—fun to have around and happy to bounce from person to person. She'll still get the "work" of the social function done without having a formal agenda for the event. Whether it's talking about the annual fund or soliciting a major gift, she'll just do it in a more "free-form" style.

Introverts can be very social, but they like to know their specific role. Whether they verbalize it or not, they tend to want to know things like "Am I doing registration?" or "What six people am I supposed to talk to?" Having specific, well-defined roles for fundraising events helps introverts feel less drained.

This can be incredibly important when dealing with donors. For example, I once worked for an organization where my two superiors were more introverted. I'm off the chart extroverted. Unfortunately, I didn't know the full impact of these distinctions at the time. I started holding alumni cultivation events in unstructured environments like brew pubs. These fit my personality so I thought they must be good for everyone—especially because the alumni seemed to have a blast.

I was shocked to find that both of my superiors found these events *very* draining. Knowing what I know now, I should have given them an outline of the event's purpose, a list of the expected participants, and the role I'd have liked them to play. Both of them were gifted fundraisers and great with people, but their manner was different from mine. I also should have interspersed these informal events with more formal ones (like a sit-down dinner). My guess is that we would have more effectively served the alumni, too. I bet introverted folks didn't come to the brew pubs for the same reasons my supervisors stopped going!

Highlands: Generalist and Specialist
According to the research done by the Highland Company, about 75% of the population is composed of "generalists"; the remaining 25% are "specialists." When you ask a *generalist* what she does, she

tends to tell you in terms of what her organization does, "Well, we help feed kids in central Africa." A *specialist* answering the same question will say, "I make sure that donors are cultivated appropriately and stewarded well." The specialist describes her personal, specific duties, not the overall team goals.

A generalist is like a casserole—all the ingredients are blended to form an end product. Most of the specific ingredients are not distinguishable in the final product. A specialist is like a Waldorf salad. All the ingredients are separately definable—the lettuce, the walnuts, the apple slices, etc. And each of these separate elements makes a distinct end product without losing their distinctiveness.

If generalists are a mile wide and an inch deep, specialists are an inch wide and a mile deep. If you've asked the donor prospect, "What do you do?" and she answers in terms of her specific duties, you know you're probably talking to a specialist. She may not know about a lot of things but what she knows, she knows *very* well. So focus the conversation on areas that will let the specialist showcase her individualized knowledge. Specialists *love* showing off what they know. (As a specialist myself, I've written this book partly for that very reason!)

Knowing whether your prospect is a generalist or a specialist can also help you determine how much detail to give about your organization. Specialists will probably prefer to get to know one aspect of your organization in great detail. Generalists will tend to be inspired by a broad overview. This knowledge will help you create the most effective solicitation strategy. Specialists will probably prefer to be very specific and strategic in their gifts; generalists will probably be more comfortable with fewer restrictions. In thinking about how to thank donors, consider that specialists might prefer being highlighted as individuals where generalists might be pleased to be seen as part of an important team.

Highlands: Classification and Concept Organization

Two more talents identified by the Highlands are *classification* and *concept organization*. High *classification* people are those who tend to love chaos and prefer to fly by the seat of their pants. They can walk into a situation and immediately spot the problems. Low classification people, on the other hand, tend to need some more structure. They need to do some analysis before pointing out where the problems may be.

People high in *concept organization* can organize everything in their head. People lower in concept organization tend to rely on planners and filing cabinets. They need lots of props to help them organize their concepts. Both classification and concept organization are crucial in asking for money.

If you're high in *classification*, you can almost instantly zoom in on what's important when talking with a potential donor. You don't really know how, but you just do it. If you're not high in classification, you won't be as good at winging it. You should create a process to help you ease into the solicitation and discover the person's hot buttons. (I've tried to leave my Get R.E.A.L. process open enough for high classification types but structured enough for those wanting a system.)

The higher you are in *concept organization*, the easier it is for you to make things quickly understandable to others. When people ask a question, you find it easy to explain even difficult concepts. The lower you are in concept organization, the more time and effort such an explanation will take. You probably need to take more time preparing your story before going into a solicitation, but you're still very successful at fundraising. You may need pictures of the people you're helping or of the buildings you want to construct in order to begin the process.

This knowledge can also come in handy when you are making solicitations. For example, if your prospects are high in classification, you need to be able to move through your presentation quickly. They rapidly grasp the ideas you're presenting, and they're ready to move on to the next point (often before you are). Don't bore them—keep moving. You're not trying to convert them to your cause; you're trying to move them towards making a gift. Conversion can happen later. For now, keep them interested.

On the other hand, if you're too fast with a person lower in classification, you risk sounding like a con artist. That's never an effective way to raise money ethically! Slow down a bit. Take more time explaining things. Sure, you want to ask for a gift, but you also would like to form a life-long relationship between your donor and your nonprofit.

What if your potential donor is low in concept organization? Again, having props and pictures like those discussed in the "Ask" step of the Get R.E.A.L. process will be helpful—even if you don't personally need them. Having an outline that you're working through which includes a step-by-step process for making the case and leading to the ask might be good. But if your prospect is really good at explaining things, she's probably higher in concept organization, so you'll want to stick less rigidly to your outline.

Highlands: Verbal and Tonal memory

We could go through all 19 abilities, but we won't. For the last set, let's look at *verbal memory* and *tonal memory*. The Highlands defines *verbal memory* as the ability to take in written information. If you're low in verbal memory, reading something isn't the best way for you to remember the information. *Tonal memory* is defined as your ability to take in information by listening to it. People high in tonal memory can hear a lecture or audio book and easily remember the content for months or years.

If you're high in tonal memory, you can take in information without taking notes. My sister is very high in tonal memory; she used to knit in her college physics classes! She said the knitting helped her (even more than note-taking) to focus and listen!

Letters and brochures are great for people high in verbal memory. They read the text and remember what they've read. But what about your donors who are high in tonal memory? Your well-crafted letters just don't work for them. Perhaps coming to an in-person event with speakers would be a better fit. Or maybe it would be good to augment your mailings with a periodic audio recording (CD or podcast) from your CEO. Or even a quick video recording posted on your site and emailed to them.

We've only looked at a few of the more than 15 talents the Highlands identifies. By now you may be asking yourself, "How is *all this information* supposed to make it *easier* for me to ask for money?!" I firmly believe it will. Although you may like to think people are all the same, there are differences. As a fundraiser, you need to pay attention to these differences. With the R.E.A.L. process, you've already got the tools you need to be an effective fundraiser, even without the content in this chapter. But knowing about D.I.S.C. and natural abilities will help you become incredibly effective in asking for money *and* in growing long-term relationships with people that love your organization!

Chapter 8
Fundraising in the Bible

Fundraising has been around for a very long time. Even biblical heroes like Moses, David, Hezekiah, Nehemiah, Jesus, and Paul asked people to support God's work financially. Despite this, almost every time I've told pastors that I love asking people for money they say, "Thank God you like doing that! I hate talking about money. I'm sure glad someone enjoys it."

I really do enjoy asking people for money; asking people for money can be one of the best ministries in the world! Asking for money is a tangible way to advance the Kingdom. Jesus had more to say about money than about most other things talked about in church. Money gets right into the real stuff of a person's life. Most people commit incredible amounts of time, energy, and creativity to making money, but comparatively little effort into learning how to handle it well.

There's no greater joy than seeing people invest in something they cherish. This section isn't about financial stewardship; plenty of wonderful books on that topic are already on the market (I've listed some of those at the the end of the book). This chapter is to help give a biblical framework for asking for money. It's intended for both practitioners and volunteers. My prayer is that it will inspire millions of believers (lay and clergy) to begin the exciting journey of fundraising.

Start at the Very Beginning

As we go along this journey, it's important to see how money was raised in the Bible. Did you know that people in the Bible asked for money? Despite reading the Bible for years, I'd missed those stories. It wasn't until I came across a small booklet called "The Ministry of Fund Raising" by Whitney Kuniholm that I realized how many famous Biblical characters engaged in fundraising. In this section, we'll look at:

- Moses,

- David,

- Hezekiah,

- Nehemiah,

- Jesus, and

- Paul

I am not attempting to create a "theology" of fundraising. But I do think we can pull out some points that will help us raise money for God's work in a way pleasing to Him.

You'll get more out of this section if you read the observations with the biblical texts. You can read the passages and the observations at: http://fundraisingcoach.com/free-articles/fundraising-in-the-bible/

Moses

Read Exodus chapters 25, 35, and 36.

What an amazingly successful capital campaign! Has your organization had to restrain people from bringing more? May we all have this problem. One of the most amazing things to me about this text is the emphasis on the lack of manipulation in Moses' appeal. God clearly told Moses to "take an offering for me; from every person whose heart makes him willing" (Ex 25:1).

And Moses' solicitation (Ex 35:4-9) is exactly what God told him to ask for, word-for-word (Ex 25:3-7). He faithfully detailed the needed gifts and the ways that those gifts were to be used. The requirement that only those "whose heart makes him willing" were to give is significant. This fundraising drive came after the golden calf debacle. People could've been easily manipulated to give out of guilt. But God wasn't interested in that kind of giving. I'm impressed by the variety of gifts Moses requested. This seems to have made the giving open to more people. (Of course, they were in the desert so there wouldn't have been that much need of money!) I hadn't realized how many skills were resident in the people that had been slaves in Egypt. I'm sure this is true of our congregations and constituents.

The rabbis find a difference in "whose heart stirred him up" and "whose spirit was willing" (Ex 35:21). Those who were willing, they say, brought what was required. This is good. But those whose heart stirred them were more generous giving more than their obligation. This was the better way. The sages also criticize the leaders being mentioned later in this section. They say the leaders probably had good intentions in waiting—they wanted to make up whatever would be lacking from the people's giving—but they fell short of their position since leaders should give first. They make up for this in Numbers 7.

The people responded incredibly well to Moses' obedient solicitation. If you read all of chapter 25, you'll see the very specific detail God gave Moses concerning how the gifts were to be used. There is a similarly specific account of how the gifts were used and who led the effort in Exodus 35 and 36.

It is interesting that it's clearly records that the offering was made to the Lord, not to the tabernacle. In fact, this story is amazingly God-centered. God is present in every step of the process:

- God details the need.

- God explains how to use the supplies.

- God prompts Moses to ask for them.

- God prompts certain people to respond.

- The people give to God.

- The gifts are used to glorify God, and they're
  made by craftsmen with God–given talents.

I think that this story demonstrates the importance of seeking
God to determine your organization's needs and then faithfully
share that information with your constituents. When asked by a
leader obeying God, the people responded with more than enough
to finish the work. It also clearly shows that God is intimately
involved with every step in the solicitation.

David
Read 1 Chronicles 29:1-20.

Praise and thanksgiving are natural results of gifts given willingly.
Isn't that inspiring? Where all sorts of people answered Moses'
appeal, David's appeal seems to be directed at the leaders (1 Chron
29:9). I believe this story shows a godly way to use an individual
donor as an example for others to follow. David clearly uses his
position as an example for the other leaders to follow (1 Chron
29:5).

This approach often makes many Christians feel uncomfortable
because of Jesus' admonition in Matthew 6:1-4:

> *"Be careful not to display your righteousness merely*
> *to be seen by people. Otherwise, you have no reward*
> *with your Father in heaven. Thus whenever you do*
> *charitable giving, do not blow a trumpet before you,*
> *as the hypocrites do in synagogues and on streets so*

that people will praise them. I tell you the truth; they have their reward. But when you do your giving, do not let your left hand know what your right hand is doing, so that your gift may be in secret. And your Father, who sees in secret, will reward you.

How can we reconcile these two passages of Scripture? This section is the beginning of Jesus correcting the three major practices of the life of the Pharisees: almsgiving, prayer, and fasting. Although Jesus repeatedly commends the practice of tithing, He never says to do it privately. In fact, He had His disciples watch people publicly give their gifts at the Temple and praised the gift of the widow and her two mites.

I'm indebted to Pastor Frank Siciliano for pointing out to me that in this passage, Jesus is instructing His disciples with a lesson familiar in rabbinic teaching: giving should never be done at the expense of the recipient. According to Second Temple Period scholar David Bivin, Mishna states there was a "secret chamber" at the Temple for the giving and receiving of alms (Shekalim 5:6). This practice enabled the recipients of alms to retain their dignity.

If you're giving alms (to the poor) to be seen by people, you're humiliating the recipient of your gift. You're robbing them of their dignity. God has no patience for that. You're giving to be puffed up at the expense of another. People that do that "have their reward" (Mt 6:2).

It's interesting to note that Jesus does not tell us to avoid doing our acts of righteousness before men. He tells us not to do them "merely to be seen by people." Obviously, the motivation of the heart is key (1 Chron 29:17).

David's prayer shows the lack of pride in his presentation. Once again, God is the source and recipient of all giving. "But who am I and who are my people, that we should be in a position to contribute this much? Indeed, everything comes from you, and we have simply given back to you what is yours." (2 Chron 29:14). He knows he's dependent on God for all he has. The leaders didn't give to David or the temple; they gave "delighted with their donations" and "contributed to the Lord with a willing attitude" (2 Chron 29:9).

Rather than trying to garner praise, David gives praise to God and leads the people in praising God. Not only did he leverage his position to influence the leaders, but also he set the example of an older generation fundraising on behalf of a younger generation (1 Chron 29:1).

Hezekiah
Read 2 Chronicles 31.

Again, we see a leader leading! This is the first of our examples to refer to "tithing." Though tithing became a temple tax, tithing is an ancient practice that predates the temple as seen in Abraham's giving a tenth of the spoils of war to Melchizedek (Gen 14:20). Did you notice the same themes being repeated in this story?

- People were freely giving.
- Gifts were being "heaped" up.
- More than enough was coming in.

This went on for four months!

So much came in that they had to build storehouses to keep it all! What's interesting here is that Hezekiah, a "secular" leader, publicly takes up the cause of the temple and the priests. Wouldn't it be great if lay leaders in the congregation made a public stand for the support and welfare of their pastors and their pastors' families? What if, like Hezekiah, they publicly announced their financial commitment in front of the congregation? I bet we'd see less pastor burnout, more mortgages on church properties paid off, and full funding for Kingdom-expanding initiatives.

Nehemiah

Read Nehemiah chapters 1 and 2.

This account is an example of pagan resources being used for God's purposes. As in all the stories so far, God is involved in the entire process: preparation, solicitation, favorable response, and successful completion.

Isn't it nice that Nehemiah lets us into his mind? This is our first look at asking from the solicitor's point of view. Here, for the first time, we see fasting as a way of preparing for a solicitation. We also see him praying that God would grant them favor.

I appreciate Nehemiah's candor. Isn't it great that he says, "this made me very fearful" (Neh 2:2)? Anyone who's asked for money has been scared! Even in his fear, he is incredibly bold. When he gets the promise of safe travel, he goes on to ask for the materials to accomplish his objective. Once again, the response was more than enough. Not only did the king agree, but he also sent a small army with Nehemiah. Some commentators see this royal escort as an indication that the king even promoted him to the position of a royal governor! Nehemiah prayerfully and boldly asks for the resources to accomplish God's work. He risks death but is rewarded with abundant provision. God's favor is amazing!

This story includes a key to Nehemiah's wisdom—he keeps many of his thoughts to himself. He even conducts an assessment of the project privately by himself (Neh 2:11-16). Once he has first-hand familiarity with the details of the task, he solicits the help of the people with him. His solicitation includes a clear statement of the need and a testimony about God's favor already evident in this project. Once again the people respond positively and immediately.

I think this story points to the legitimacy of asking non-Christians and the government to invest in Kingdom work. It also highlights the need for fundraisers to continually seek God and ask for His favor before and during solicitations. God is the prime mover in the fundraising process. Our requests are to build up His kingdom.

Jesus

Read Luke 8:1-3.

This passage doesn't show Jesus appealing for support, but it does show that He and the Twelve received donor support. As a fundraiser, these few verses are comforting to me. Even if I'm raising money that will (in part) pay for my work, I know Jesus received support for his work too. It seems striking to me that these women would be able to help "out of their own means" (Luke 8:3). In this culture, women were largely seen as property of their husbands or fathers, but they must have had some sort of "resources" in order to be able to give. This points to Jesus being truly open to relating to everyone—not just the poor but the rich as well. (Isn't it wonderfully ironic that some of Jesus' provision came from Herod's household?)

Paul

Read: 1 Corinthians 16:1-4
2 Corinthians 8 and 9
Philippians 4:10-20
1 Timothy 6:17-19

Paul certainly has a lot to say about giving. The following is in no way meant to be an exhaustive study of the approaches he used and all the theological implications that can be derived from his writing. As with the previous stories, I simply want to draw out some of the observations my clients and I have made about his approach to asking for money.

First, Paul is using a format very common to us today—a donor appeal letter. The passage from 1 Corinthians shows a reasoned, logical, proportional approach to systematic giving (1 Cor 16:2). Such systematic giving seems reminiscent of today's monthly contribution programs.

The portion from 2 Corinthians seems to be inspired in part due to a stalled fundraising campaign (2 Cor 8:11; 9:3). The Corinthians made a significant pledge, but they haven't fulfilled it yet. Interestingly, by bragging about the Macedonian churches, Paul employs competition to inspire the Corinthians to fulfill their pledge (2 Cor 8:1). Similar to the account of the tabernacle, there is a detailed description concerning the careful administration of the gift. Paul highlights the integrity of the process and the integrity of the people handling it (2 Cor 8:19).

Paul uses powerful writing skills that seem to me to border on manipulation. But he is quick to note (as is true with the previous examples) that giving to God's work is to be done willingly and generously (2 Cor 8:8; 9:5, 7). He claims not to be commanding them to give but "testing the genuineness of their love" (2 Cor 8:8). He even states that giving is a sign of "your obedience to your confession in the gospel of Christ" (2 Cor 9:13).

I appreciate Paul's reassurance "I am not saying this because I am in need" (Phil 4:11). It seems to me that any ministry that regularly employs crisis tactics to raise funds should reexamine the integrity in doing so.

For me, Paul's instructions on how to ask for money in the passage from 1 Timothy are a nice counterbalance to James' exhortation not to show favoritism (James 2:1-12). As Christians, we're not to show people favor based on their net worth. Still, we need to be good stewards of our organization's limited resources. I think that fundraisers will always live in the tension between not showing favoritism and encouraging the rich to be "generous to others."

Review and Application

Those of us who are fundraisers are amazingly blessed. We get to follow in the footsteps of some incredible people of faith. We get to be part of a process saturated with God's hand. And the natural result of doing our job well is people bursting out in praise and thanksgiving and abundantly supplying the need.

The following is a brief review of points that we can draw from the examples we've observed. The list is always growing, so please let me know of your own additions. I can be reached at marc@ fundraisingcoach.com.

- Ask God for His perspective on the need.
- Relay that perspective faithfully.
- Seek gifts only from those giving with a willing heart.
- Use your own giving as well as other donors' giving as public examples.
- Make sure God is the center of all of your fundraising efforts.
- Fast, pray, and ask for His favor.
- Be ready for the incredible release of joy and praise at the outpouring from God's people when they're asked God's way.
- Ask boldly from believers and nonbelievers alike.

- There's no shame involved in accepting donor support—even Jesus did.

- It's appropriate to use a mix of solicitation methods including face-to-face visits and solicitation letters.

- Encourage people to set up some form of systematic giving.

- Talk about the tithe. It's no longer a Temple tax, but it is still a helpful measure of giving.

- Give praise to God for His faithfulness.

Summary

"Remember the words of the Lord Jesus, how he said, it is more blessed to give than to receive."

         - Acts 20:35

"We ourselves feel that what we are doing is just a drop in the ocean. But the ocean would be less because of that missing drop."

         - Mother Teresa

"A generous man will prosper; he who refreshes others will be refreshed."

         - Proverbs 11:25

"The price of living is giving."
         - Unknown

"It is only in the giving of oneself to others that we truly live."

         - Ethel Percy Andrus

"We make a living by what we get, but we make a life by what we give."

— Winston Churchill

"No person was ever honored for what he received. Honor has been the reward for what he gave."

— Calvin Coolidge

"Giving opens the way for receiving."

— Florence Scovel Shinn

"I have found that among its other benefits, giving liberates the soul of the giver."

— Maya Angelou

"Apart from the ballot box, philanthropy presents the one opportunity the individual has to express his meaningful choice over the direction in which our society will progress."

— George G. Kirstein

Congratulations! You've reached the end of the book! You are much better equipped to raise money for your ministry!

You've learned detailed ways to go about the Get R.E.A.L. process: Research, Engage, Ask, and Love. You've explored the seven biggest mistakes we make when trying to raise money. You've learned that putting yourself in the donor's shoes can make your fundraising exponentially more successful. Finally, you've been introduced to a couple of great tools to help you relate with other people more effectively and ask them to support your nonprofit using an approach that's tailored to them.

That's it. You're finished with the book. But you're only just beginning your journey.

One of my favorite quotes from Glenn Bland's classic book *Success, the Glenn Bland Method* is:

> "Shoot for the moon and if you miss, you can hit the eagle. Shoot for the eagle and miss, you'll hit the ground."

Setting high goals is an important thing. When working with a nonprofit, you don't necessarily want to trumpet the highest goals. Nothing is more demoralizing than announcing that you fell way short of your goals. But, you must get over your fear of what might happen. Be tenacious in going after big gifts. The Kingdom of God is worth it. If you don't ask, you'll never know!

Use the R.E.A.L. steps. Better yet, gather your colleagues and teach the steps to them. You'll remember much better if you try to teach these four steps to someone this week.

Please drop me a line if I can be of assistance.
My email is marc@fundraisingcoach.com.

Appendix
Get R.E.A.L. Tools

Research

David Lamb's Prospect Research Page
http://lambresearch.com/

Google.com

University of Vermont's Research Tools Page
http://www.uvm.edu/~prospect/index.html

Blackbaud Analytics http://www.blackbaud.com/

WealthEngine.com http://wealthengine.com/

GiftRangeCalculator.com
http://www.GiftRangeCalculator.com/

Blackbaud Gift Range Calculator
https://www.blackbaud.com/nonprofit-resources/gift-range-calculator.aspx

Engage

The Millionaire Next Door by Thomas Stanley and William Danko (1998)
http://amzn.to/KWTMXF

Endless Referrals by Bob Burg
http://amzn.to/NFop3Q

The Anatomy of Buzz by Emmanuel Rosen
http://amzn.to/M99JfH

Creating Customer Evangelists by Jackie Huba and Ben McConnell
http://amzn.to/KWUfcj

Who's Telling YOUR Story? by Marc A. Pitman
http://amzn.to/LstDGl

Ask

Asking by Jerry Panas
http://amzn.to/Ph6dnk

50 Asks in 50 Days by Amy Eisenstein
http://amzn.to/Ox4CIR

AskingMatters.com Asking Style Profile
http://www.askingmatters.com/find-your-asking-style/

The Ask Without Fear! DVD series
http://www.FundraisingCoachDVDs.com/

The Self-Guided Ask Without Fear Full Day Retreat
http://www.BoardRetreatPacks.com/

Love

How to Win Friends and Influence People by Dale Carnegie
http://amzn.to/LSgYdK

Growing Givers' Hearts by Thomas Jeavons and Rebekah Burch Basinger
http://amzn.to/RnT7Dh

Love is the Killer App by Tim Sanders
http://amzn.to/Ph8FKH

Fundraising for Ministry and The Ministry of Fundraising

Friend Raising: Building a Missionary Support Team That Lasts by Betty J. Barnett
http://amzn.to/1MqAd9n

Funding Your Ministry: An In-depth, Biblical Guide for Successfully Raising Personal Support by Scott Morton
http://amzn.to/1MqAbOG

The God Ask: A Fresh Biblical Approach to Personal Support Raising by Steve Shadrach
http://amzn.to/1GHaB68

God and Mammon: Asking for Money in the New Testament by Jouette M. Bassler
http://amzn.to/1K8NpOo

Godly Materialism: Rethinking Money and Possessions by John Schneider
http://amzn.to/1ZDcMDl

God and Your Stuff: The Vital Link Between Your Possessions and Your Soul by Wesley K. Willmer
http://amzn.to/1ZDcRaf

People Raising: A Practical Guide to Raising Funds by William P. Dillon
http://amzn.to/1K8OcyN

The Ministry of Fund Raising by Whitney Kuniholm, Prison Fellowship Ministries, 1990.

"Oral Torah: Tithing." by David Bivin
http://jerusalemperspective.com/ [Premium membership may be required but is well worth it!]

A Spirituality of Fundraising by Henri J.M. Nouwen
http://amzn.to/1K8OUMw

Other Tools

Movie Mondays: free weekly videos to help you with your fundraising
http://www.MovieMondays2.com/

Life is Tremendous by Charlie "Tremendous" Jones
http://amzn.to/M8byrM

Success: The Glenn Bland Method by Glenn Bland
http://amzn.to/KWWpsn

Highlands Ability Battery
http://fundraisingcoach.com/highlands.htm

DISC http://www.personality-insights.com/

Marc A. Pitman

About the Author

An international leadership coach and fundraising trainer, Marc A. Pitman, helps nonprofit board members and staff get excited about asking for money. He is the founder of The Concord Leadership Group; he also created FundraisingCoach. com which is recognized by The Atlantic as "1 of 5 Philanthropic blogs fundraisers *need* to read." He is the author of *Ask Without Fear!*, the executive director of The Nonprofit Academy (an affordable fundraising training program), and an Advisory Panel member of Rogare (a prestigious international fundraising think tank).

His first book *Ask Without Fear!*® has been translated into Polish, Dutch, Spanish, and Mandarin. Marc also speaks to groups around the world and at conferences like the World Fundraising Summit in Mexico the Association for Fundraising Professionals International. His dynamic trainings even attract groups like the International Bowling Expo. Because of his experience in nonprofit fundraising and leadership training as well as his balanced commentary, he has appeared as a guest on various media venues (TV, radio, and print) as diverse as Al Jazeera, SUCCESS Magazine, and Fox News.

With a passion that's made people call him the "Johnny Appleseed of fundraising," Marc believes fundraising is all about leadership. Fundraising affects—every aspect of an organization mission, vision, board governance, HR, marketing, and community relations. So he is committed to making it ridiculously easy for everyone (board members, volunteers, and nonprofit staff) to get fundraising training. Marc continues to write books, create fundraising training DVDs, and collaborate on systems like *100 Donors in 90 Days*.

Marc's leadership experience also includes planting and pastoring a Vineyard church, managing a gubernatorial campaign, teaching internet marketing at both the undergraduate and graduate level, and being chosen as one of Maine's first "40 Under Forty," honoring Maine's emerging generation of leaders.

He is the husband of his best friend and the father of three amazing kids. And if you see him drive by, he'll probably be singing 80's tunes loud enough to embarrass his family.

Find Marc online at:

Twitter: http://twitter.com/marcapitman

LinkedIn: http://linkedin.com/in/marcapitman

Facebook: http://facebook.com/askwithoutfear

**To sign up for his free email newsletter go to
http://FundraisingCoach.com/.**

Ask Without Fear!®

Get the internationally acclaimed book that started it all.

Marc Pitman wrote *Ask Without Fear!*® because there were so many initiatives that could make the world a better place if only they had the funding. So he distilled his years of successful fundraising experience into a fun, practical book ideal for board members and volunteers.

Ask Without Fear! DVD

Marc went into the studio to record the content of *Ask Without Fear!*® for a nonprofit's to use in training their board or staff.

Broken into question-and-answer segments, this series can be viewed in one sitting or referenced when needed.

**Get both the book and
the DVD on Amazon or at
www.FundraisingCoach.com**

BOARD RETREAT *Party* PACK

INCLUDES:

1 - "Ask Without Fear" DVD - Includes the get R.E.A.L. training videos
1 - "Ask Without Fear" Resource CD
5 - Board Retreat plan, checklist, and instructional sheets
10 - "Ask Without Fear" Books

More information at
www.BoardRetreatPacks.com

Bulk Orders

To order 10 or more copies for your board or next conference, or to book Marc to speak at your next event, contact him at:

Mail: The Concord Leadership Group LLC
           2435 East North Street, Ste 1108-171
           Greenville, SC 29615

Phone: (317) 296-7886

E-mail: marc@concordleadershipgroup.com

Website: www.FundraisingCoach.com
           www.TheNonprofitAcademy.com
           www.TheConcordLeadershipGroup.com

Notes

Notes

Notes

CPSIA information can be obtained
at www.ICGtesting.com
Printed in the USA
FSHW020731090219
55505FS